Family Secrets

Family Secrets

The Khan Family Cookbook
by

Zarine Khan

Photographs and Food Styling
Ashima Narain

Lustre Press
Roli Books

Acknowledgements

I am immensely grateful to my dearest mother-in-law for giving me most of her recipes which I have now passed on to all of you, along with the other recipes that I have picked up through my Parsi lineage.

I would like to thank the publisher of this book, Priya Kapoor, who has worked hard behind the scenes, and would also like to give special thanks to the photographer Ashima Narain for making it a picture-perfect home-cooked cuisine book. Lastly, thanks to all my family members who have encouraged and forced me to get this book printed. I love them all.

Dedication

······················

I would like to dedicate this book to the late Bibi Fatima Begum Khan, my dear mother-in-law. She was the one who helped me acquire a taste for good home-cooked food. She also opened my eyes to the fact that simple *ghar-ka-khana* can often turn out to be far better than recipes that are elaborate, time consuming, and look good in presentation only.

The lasting popularity of our Khan-household food prompted me to write this simple book of home recipes. I hope you enjoy these dishes as much as our friends have.

L-R: Myself with grandson Azaan, Sussanne with son Hrehaan, Malaika, Zayed with Adah and Hridaan, Farah with daughter Fizaa, Simone and Sanjay with Zayed's son Zidaan.

My four children. L-R are Sussanne Khan, Farah Khan, and Simone Arora. Seated at the centre is my son, Zayed.

Contents

Introduction

As a fourteen-year-old girl, I remember living a charmed life. I was in the ninth grade and was surrounded by loving friends and family. I loved to eat the Parsi meals of my parental home, and my love for sports such as netball and throw ball ensured that I could eat as much dhansak as I wanted to without worrying about my weight! My family and I lived in the private Jussawala Wadi compound in Juhu, which was a stone's throw away from the beach. Every morning, whilst walking to my school bus stop, I passed a house where a fair, elderly lady sat on the balcony of her flat and she would give me a wide smile and a friendly wave. Shortly, I began to look forward to the morning greetings from Fatima Bibi, for I felt she was responsible for making my day a pleasant one – like a lucky charm. Little did I imagine then that this very lady would be my dear mother-in-law in the near future!

Fatima Bibi and her five sons, the handsome Khan Brothers – Feroz, Abbas, Shahrooq, Sameer, and Akbar, along with their beautiful sister Dilshad, had become my neighbours. Though originally from Bangalore, they had shifted residence as the eldest son, Feroz, was keen on coming to Mumbai to pursue his star-studded ambitions. These handsome guys had brought with them a great deal of excitement to the otherwise staid environment of our wadi, and many young maidens would have a field day in trying to get their attention!

When I happened to pass by their house, these young lads would mischievously whistle at me from their balcony to the tune of famous Sergeant Major's March, which was a theme from a Hollywood film called *The Bridge on the River Kwai.* Yet, one amongst them would refrain from doing so. When I felt compelled to look up, I saw a lean, fair, and tall lad with a mane of luscious dark hair watching me intently. He reminded me of the famous actor George Chakaris from the popular film, *The West Side Story.* I have to admit, I was taken by his personality. Yet, being of a timid **nature**, I would instantly lower my head and walk away at an even faster pace while the other brothers continued to whistle in tune with the pace of my steps!

But 'Destiny' had decided to play its part! For on one beautiful Sunday morning, when one of my girlfriends and I decided to take a long walk along the shoreline of Juhu Beach, we were pleasantly surprised to see this same boy strolling ahead of us! I nudged my friend, 'That's my neighbour. The one who keeps giving me those intent stares.' Just then, as if by some form of telepathy, he chose to turn around. On seeing us from a distance, he picked up a stray twig lying on the beach and scribbled on the wet sand. He then glanced over at us, as if daring us to come and read it. My friend made me hasten our pace to reach that spot before a wave washed his words away. Fortunately, we were just in time to read the single word he wrote: 'Hullo'. Being young and inexperienced, I was perplexed as what to do! But my courageous friend had picked up the same stick and wrote on my behalf a simple 'Hullo'. On seeing her do this, I got even more nervous and insisted that we turn back instantly for our home. After protesting for a bit, she finally listened to my plea. But as we were walking back towards the entrance of our wadi, we heard a deep voice from behind us say, 'May I join you?' On turning around, I stared into the handsome eyes of my neighbour. Before I could even utter a single word, my friend replied in the affirmative. And that was the beginning of my love story!

His name was Abbas, and he was just eighteen years of age then, with dreams reaching up to the stars! I was happy to attach myself to a boyfriend just to be included in my gang of friends at school, who all professed to have steady boyfriends. We both were very young and madly in love! Through the ups and downs of our relationship, we continued to go steady for seven years, visualizing many high dreams, of which a few even came crashing down! Yet, we held on together and continued our friendship till at last my youthful boyfriend became an overnight movie star with his first two films, *Dosti* and *Haqeeqat*, becoming silver jubilee hits. By then, my steady boyfriend had acquired the screen name of Sanjay. Satyen Bose, the director of *Dosti*, was behind his name change, as he felt that this new name suited my boyfriend's sunny smile!

ABOVE: *My parents, Burjor and Sheroo Katrak.* FACING PAGE: *Myself, when I was aged ten.*

We were married in 1966 when I was just twenty and my handsome husband was twenty-four years of age.

During our courtship years, I would visit his house almost every day as my mother-in-law doted on me. She was Persian by birth, married to a Pathan named Sadiq Ali Khan, and their genetic combination had produced such good-looking children. After my father-in-law had expired, this young widow had the onus of bringing up all of her six children single-handedly. She was a fantastic cook. Thus whenever I visited their home, I would instantly get a whiff of the exotic dishes she prepared for her family.

Being a foodie and lover of good cuisine, I enjoyed whatever my mother-in-law would serve me, and she in turn was happy to see me devour her food with such relish. My constant praise for her cooking would encourage her to make me sample more of her dishes. This was my first experience of relishing Mughlai and Persian cuisine, and I ate to my heart's content! Fortunately, I had a high metabolic rate and so I never put on extra pounds in spite of consuming so much of her delicious food. Sometimes I would have double-meals just to taste another bite of my mother-in-law's cooking and I could see the smile of contentment on her face. One day, I was encouraged to take a paper and pen and jot down all of her delicious recipes. Over time, I had become extremely close to my beautiful mother-in-law and in the process, I acquired a treasure trove of her home-cooked recipes!

As I came from an aristocratic Parsi background – the Katrak family – I was accustomed to good Parsi food right from childhood. Dishes like mutton dhansak and patra-ni-macchi were the staple food of my growing-up years. My family followed the tradition of eating together as we were a very close-knit family, and food helped in keeping us even more bonded. So it was easy for me to adapt into the Khan household, the members of which were also very attached to each other and bonded similarly over good food.

Soon, my taste buds jumped from Parsi cuisine into Mughlai and Persian food. When I tried my mother-in-law's cooking for the first time, I noticed a slight tangy flavour which was influenced by her years of living in the southern city of Bangalore. She would use a little tamarind and give her dishes a twist which was quite different from our Parsi cuisine. But I adapted to this taste fast. In fact, I loved this new flavour.

ABOVE: *The Khan family. L-R: Sanjay, Shahrooq, Akbar, Bibi Fatima Begum, Sameer, Feroz, and Dilshad.* BELOW: *My husband Sanjay, and myself right after our wedding, pictured here with my mother-in-law and young nieces-in-law.* FACING PAGE ABOVE: *With friends at my pre-wedding mehendi ceremony. My friend kisses me, while my mother (seated extreme right) looks on.* FACING PAGE BELOW: *At my wedding reception. L-R are my brother-in-law Feroz, myself, and Sanjay.*

There were many firsts that I was introduced to by my mother-in-law's cooking. I was surprised to learn that a lot of the mouth-watering recipes came about from mixing meat with vegetables, such as tinda gosht, bhendi gosht, cabbage gosht, and many more. I realized that veggies tasted even better when mixed with meat. Of course, she had a host of other even more special recipes such as her different types of biryanis. There was the Bangalori

biryani, dum-ki-biryani, kheema biryani, veggie biryani, masala rice biryani, and chop pulau. The variety in her recipes never ceased to amaze me and all her dishes turned out to be exceptional and exotic. She taught me the art of complementing one dish with another, and made sure that the table had a variety of colour so as to whet one's visual appetite. Thus, no two similar-coloured dishes would be placed together when she set her table. If there was a red mutton dish, she would place a green-coloured dish beside it.

My mother-in-law had a tradition of keeping an open kitchen which to date I follow in my own home. Hence, since I've been married, our kitchen fire has never been put out even for a single day! Food is cooked for our staff daily in our kitchen even when we are away for a holiday. My husband describes this as *barkat* – he believes we are fortunate to have guests who come and eat in our home; and he feels that feeding people brings us an abundance of goodwill and good luck.

Thus over time, collecting newer recipes became my passion and hobby. When I was invited to any of my Parsi relative's homes and I found a particular

dish that was special, I would make it a point to get that recipe. I chose recipes that were simple to make, delicious to taste, and light on the stomach. I preferred not to use cashewnuts or heavy creams for flavour. After adding many more such recipes, I decided to have those typed, and bound because I considered it to be a valuable treasure of simple, home-cooked food. Never did I imagine that this would someday turn out to be my very own cookbook of simple home cooking!

CLOCKWISE FROM LEFT:
A young Feroz seated beside my late father-in-law, Sadiq Ali Khan; Sanjay's autographed picture, taken shortly after he became an overnight star; Myself, aged sixteen; Sanjay photographed with Meena Kumari at our wedding reception; My sister-in-law Dilshad and her husband Javed at their wedding reception, photographed here with Sanjay and Shahrooq.

CLOCKWISE FROM LEFT: *My daughter Sussanne, aged four, dressed as a Kashmiri belle; Sanjay and I celebrating the derby victory of our horse Prince Khartoum (Feroz can be seen in the background, shaking a leg with Parmeshwar Godrej); My daughter Farah, aged nine, in Kashmiri garb; My son Zayed, aged six, dressed as a Kashmiri lad; Celebrations at our home, L-R: Parmesh, Mumtaz, my brother-in-law Sameer, with Parveen Babi and Kamini Kaushal; My daughter Simone, aged eight, dressed in a Kashmiri costume; L-R: Sanjay, Dilip Kumar, Saira Banu, and myself.*

17

Toasting with friends. Pictured L-R: Sir Ramgoolam, the then prime minister of Mauritius, Sanjay, film distributor Mr. Shankar, the cinema legend Raj Kapoor and his wife Krishna, Feroz, with producer Nari Sippy. **FACING PAGE ABOVE:** *Friends at our home. L-R: Poet-lyricist Anand Bakshi and composer R.D. Burman, Sanjay, Sir Ramgoolam, Sanjeev Kumar, and some of our family friends.* **FACING PAGE BELOW:** *Actor Kabir Bedi, former chief minister of Maharashtra Y.B. Chavan, and myself photographed at our annual Iftar party.*

From the early days of my marriage, we entertained a large number of important persons and dignitaries as most were eager to meet a Bollywood family. Due to my husband being the first Hindi movie producer to film in the beautiful island of Mauritius – whilst filming our own film *Chandi Sona* in 1977, we had the opportunity to meet the Mauritian Prime Minister and invite him to our home. Soon after that, numerous Indian and world figures such as the King and Queen of Nepal, and the King of Morocco and a host of others, became our friends too. They would all confess to have had one of the best meals at my house, which of course included our famous biryani. Whenever we entertained these prominent dignitaries, I never catered from restaurants and especially made it a point to serve our very own home-cooked food, and all my guests simply relished and devoured to their heart's content. Even the late Sunil Dutt was a great fan of our green masala pomfret. I recall when he was in hospital, he had requested me to get that for him, and I remember smuggling the fish through the hospital's strict security rules!

Steadily, word spread around, and our home cuisine got to be acclaimed by one and all. Besides our biryanis, the shammi kebabs, and the bagara baingan were also in great demand. Friends and acquaintances would want to be invited to our house, just to experience our famous cuisine. I was elated by their reactions and this gave me the incentive to keep adding more recipes to my bound self-made cookbook. I felt confident about the fact that if my cook ever decided to leave, I could easily train another person with this handy cookbook. Yet, I must add, that not a single member of my staff has ever willfully wanted to leave our household, and we are known to maintain most of our staff right up to their retirement age!

Our Eid parties at home would usually be a gathering of family and a few close friends. The highlight would be my mother-in-law's recipes of her famous biryanis. At the dinner table, my family members like to talk, and hold long discussions and we often resemble a loud-talking Italian family – as we continue to voice out our views on various topics, from history to politics, in our overpowering voices! Needless to say, no cell phones are allowed whilst we are at the dinner table.

Sadly, this book does not contain any desserts, because I had once a Parsi friend who loved desserts so much and was so obese, that just seeing her gobble up the many sweet dishes after each meal at her home, made me

promise to myself that I would never get my kids into the habit of a sweet tooth. Hence I never made desserts in our home, except on festive occasions. Instead I made fresh fruits our dessert.

As time passed, my four kids grew up enjoying the delicious dishes from this very cookbook. In fact, all the special food served during my children's

ABOVE: *Zayed's first birthday party. L-R: Tanya Godrej, my mother, Zayed, myself, and Farah.*
BELOW: *An affectionate moment between Farah and Simone.*

wedding celebrations was also home-cooked, and this included our family biryani! After their respective marriages, they would miss our home food so much that they would request me to send their favourite dishes to their residences regularly. This was only possible **as** we lived at a distance of 5 minutes apart.

By the grace of God, I have now got nine grandkids between the ages of two and nineteen, and all of them just adore our family food. 'Nana and Nani's house food is the best!' they proclaim. Some of their favourite dishes include the Parsi pepper mutton, fish patia, meat khichra, and of course the good old biryani which is our regular Sunday family fare. The second favourite is the home-cooked chicken korma! Even my nephew, Fardeen Khan, loves our food

CLOCKWISE FROM LEFT: *A moment shared with my beautiful daughters; Simone with her husband Ajay Arora and their sons Armaan and Yuraaz; Celebrating my birthday, L-R: My daughter-in-law Malaika, Zayed, myself, and Simone; On Farah's tenth wedding anniversary, L-R: Sussanne, my neice Laila, Simone, and my nephew Fardeen.*

immensely. To the degree that after eating at my place, he usually requests me to send some to his home for the next day! His favourite being the biryani and the paya. And in spite of adhering to a strict high protein diet, Hrithik loves our home food so much that his diet goes for a toss when he joins us for our family meals. My other sons-in-law, Ajay Arora and Aqeel Ali are everready to join the family dinners for their favourites such as the dahi chicken barbecue and the dum ka kheema, which is Aqeel's special.

The men in our family are also excellent cooks. They love cooking as it's a form of relaxation for them. In fact, Sanjay is also a great cook. My son Zayed has got this talent of cooking from his father and grandmother and he is also an extraordinary cook. But he prefers to stick to mainly European cuisine. Cooking can be great fun as it brings the family together, and helps us in spending time together.

ABOVE: *Farah and her husband Aqeel Ali at their tenth wedding anniversary celebrations in Goa.* BELOW: *Actor Sanjay Dutt congratulating Zayed and Malaika on their wedding day.*

ABOVE: *In Europe with my grandsons Yuraaz and Armaan.*
BELOW: *Sussanne with her second-born Hridaan.*

When my kids entertain in their own homes, they usually ask my cook to come over and prepare some of our famous dishes for their guests. Thus I decided to make copies of my cookbook and give each of them one, so that they could prepare these recipes in their own homes and carry our culinary traditions forward to their future generations.

At one of these dinners in my daughter Sussanne's home, whilst a guest relished our food, he said to her, 'It would be a shame if your mom did not publish these recipes'. When Sussanne encouraged me to do so, at first I was a bit hesitant. But when all my other kids also urged me on, I asked myself: 'Why not?'

Thus I am immensely grateful to my dearest mother-in-law Bibi Fatima Begum, for giving me most of these special recipes. I have now passed on this to you, along with some of the other recipes that I have picked up through my Parsi lineage.

This book contains a merry mix of recipes from Mughlai, Persian, Continental, and Parsi cuisine. It is a collection of wholesome, simple, and tasty home-cooked food. So my dear readers, I sincerely hope you do try out all the recipes and enjoy them as much as my family members and our guests have done through these past many years, and they all still do to this very day.

HAPPY MOMENTS WITH THE ENTIRE FAMILY: STANDING, L-R: *Yuraaz, Zayed, Hrithik, Sussanne,*
Malaika with her son Aariz, Aqueel Ali with daughter Fizaa, Farah with son Azaan, and
Ajay Arora. SITTING, L-R: *Myself with grandson Hrehaan, Sanjay with grandsons Hridaan &*
Armaan, Simone's daughter Adah, and Simone with Zayed's son Zidaan.

Vegetarian

Dahiwala Baingan

Brinjal in yoghurt

Serves 6

1 kg large   Brinjal (*baingan*)
1 cup   Beaten yoghurt (*dahi*)
1 tsp   Black pepper (*kali mirch*)
1 tsp   Ground cumin (*jeera powder*)
1 tsp   Red chilli powder (*lal mirch powder*)
Fresh coriander for garnish
Salt to taste
Oil for frying

1. Take the brinjal and cut it into round slices of ½ inch thickness.
2. Sprinkle salt on the slices. Then deep fry in a pan.
3. Once well-fried and cooked through, place the slices on paper to drain extra oil.
4. Just before serving, spread the brinjal slices out in a flat layer in a long dish.
5. Take the yoghurt and pour it over the brinjal slices.
6. Then mix some salt, black pepper, ground cumin powder, red chilli powder and finely cut fresh coriander in a bowl and sprinkle over the yoghurt and brinjal and serve.

Favourite

Zayed, my youngest
and only son has repeat
helpings whenever Red
masala Chops, Kalmiri
ka Char, and white rice
are served.

Kalmiri ka Char

Spiced tamarind gravy

Serves: 6

 *Ingredients*

Step 1

250 gms	Tamarind (*imli*) soaked in 3 tbsp water
½ litre	Water
2	Tomatoes
½ bunch	Fresh coriander (chopped *dhania pata*)
½ tsp	Red chilli powder (*lal mirch* powder)
½ tsp	Turmeric powder (*haldi* powder)
½ tsp	Coriander powder (*dhania* powder)
2 tsp	Crushed black pepper (*kali mirch* powder)
Salt to taste	

1. Soak tamarind in water, remove the pulp.

2. To the tamarind water, add tomatoes, coriander leaves, red chilli powder, turmeric powder, coriander powder, black pepper, and salt to taste. Mash together, preferably by hand, and keep aside.

Step 2

1 large	Onion (sliced)
1 tsp	Whole cumin (*jeera*)
15	Cloves garlic (mashed)
20	Curry leaves
3	Whole dried red chillies (*sabut lal mirch* – cut in two)
2 tbsp	Oil
2 tbsp	Ghee

3. Put ghee and oil in a pan. Add cumin, red chillies, curry leaves, garlic and fry for 2 minutes.

4. Add onion and fry till light brown.

5. Then add the tamarind water (Step 1), stir well and boil for 10 minutes.

6. Serve.

Stuffed Karelas

Stuffed bitter gourd

Serves: 6

For Frying:

3	Onions (chopped)
3	Dried/dry red chillies (remove seeds)
2 tbsp	Coriander seeds (*dhania* seeds)
7	Cloves garlic
1 tsp	Oil

½ kg	Bitter gourd (*karela* – remove skin and seeds)

(Add 2 tbsp salt and 2 tbsp vinegar and soak for 10 minutes. Drain.)

3 tbsp	Grated coconut
2 tbsp	Dry mango powder (*amchur* powder)
Salt to taste	

1. Fry all the ingredients for 5 minutes. Add grated coconut and keep aside. After the mixture has cooled down, grind coarsely.

2. Add *amchur* powder and salt to taste.

3. Stuff the *karelas* with this mixture.

4. Add 2 tbsp of oil on a baking tray and place the stuffed *karelas* in a flat layer on the tray. Bake for 30 minutes in a pre-heated oven at 180 degrees C.

Aloo Chakna

Spicy potato vegetable

Serves: 6

Ingredients

1 kg	Potatoes
½ kg	Tomatoes
2	Onions (chopped)
7 tbsp	Oil
1 tsp	Cumin (*jeera* seeds)
¾ tsp	Mustard (*sarson* seeds)
1 whole	Garlic pod (crushed)
20	Curry leaves
3 tsp	Red chilli powder (*lal mirch* powder)
¼ tsp	Turmeric powder (*haldi* powder)
200 gms	Yoghurt (*dahi*)
¼ bunch	Fresh coriander
5	Green Chillies (slit)
1	Lemon (juiced)
Salt to taste	

Method

1. Boil the potatoes till cooked and keep aside.
2. In a separate pan, heat oil. Add cumin, mustard, garlic, curry leaves and fry for 2 minutes. Then add the onions.
3. Stir in the tomatoes, red chilli powder, turmeric, salt and fry till tomatoes are completely cooked. Add yoghurt.
4. Peel and cut the potatoes into quarters and add to the tomato mixture.
5. Leave this on a low flame for 10 minutes. Add salt to taste.
6. Sprinkle fresh coriander, green chillies, and the lemon juice while it is on low flame.
7. When the oil surfaces, switch off the flame and serve.

Dal Pareen

A tamarind flavoured dal

Serves: 6

Ingredients

½ cup	Split yellow dal (*moong* dal)	¾ tsp	Turmeric powder (*haldi* powder)
¼ cup	Split red dal (*masoor* dal)	250 ml	Tamarind water (*imli* water)
¼ cup	Split pea dal (*channa* dal)	2 tbsp	Oil
¼ cup	Yellow pigeon pea (*tuwar* dal)	2 Medium	Onions (chopped)
4 large	Tomatoes	1 tsp	Mustard seeds (*sarson* seeds)
15	Curry leaves	1 tsp	Cumin seeds (*jeera* seeds)
10	Garlic cloves (sliced)	¼ tsp	Fenugreek seeds (*methi* seeds)
½ bunch	Fresh coriander (*dhania*)	8	Dry red chillies (*sabut lal mirch*)
2 tsp	Red chilli powder (*lal mirch* powder)	10	Garlic cloves
			Salt to taste

Method

1. Wash and soak all mixed dal for 30 minutes.

2. Then boil the dals together in a pressure cooker along with the tomatoes, curry leaves, salt, turmeric and red chilli powder.

3. After the first whistle of the cooker, reduce the heat and let it simmer for 1 or 2 more whistles.

4. Check in between and if required add 1 more cup of water to the cooker.

5. After the second whistle, let it cook for 15 minutes more on slow fire, then add the tamarind water and cook till another whistle.

6. Remove the dals and mash them with a spoon and add finely chopped coriander and keep aside.

7. In another frying pan do a *baghar* by first adding oil, then frying the onions and sliced garlic till light brown.

8. Add mustard seeds, cumin seeds, fenugreek seeds, dry red chillies, and fry with the onions.

9. When slightly browned, add the entire contents into the dal and let it all boil till it reaches a nice, slightly sticky and thick consistency. Check for seasoning.

Channe ki Dal ke Barreh

Mashed split pea fritters   *Serves: 8*

Ingredients

½ kg	Split pea dal (*channa* dal)	1 tsp	Red chilli powder
2 small	Onions (chopped)	1 tsp	Ginger-garlic paste
2 bunches	Green spring onions (*pyaaz ka patta*)		Salt to taste
			Oil for frying
1 bunch	Dill (*sui ki bhaji*)		Pinch of Soda
4	Green chillies		

Method

1. Soak *channa* dal overnight, or for at least 3 hrs. Drain and grind coarsely.

2. Add the chopped onions, spring onions, *sui ki bhaji* with its ends discarded, green chillies, red chilli powder, ginger-garlic paste, salt, and a pinch of soda, making it into small patties.

3. In a wok, heat some oil and deep fry the patties till golden brown. Serve.

Bagara Baingan

Slow-cooked baby brinjals   *Serves: 6*

Ingredients

¾ kg	Small brinjals (*baingan*)
3	Onions, sliced
3 large	Tomatoes
¼	Coconut, grated
8	Green chillies, whole
7	Kashmiri chillies (*sabut lal mirch*) without seeds
¼ bunch	Fresh coriander, chopped
10-15	Curry leaves
2 tsp	Fenugreek (*methi*) seeds
5 tbsp	Oil
2 tsp	Mustard (*sarson*) seeds
7	Garlic flakes
2 tsp	Ginger-garlic paste
3 tbsp	Coriander (*dhania*) powder
1 tsp	Red chilli (*lal mirch*) powder
¼ tsp	Turmeric (*haldi*) powder
50 gms	Tamarind (*imli*) soaked in water
Salt to taste	

Method

1. Fry the brinjal and keep aside.
2. In 1 tbsp of oil, fry sliced onions, Kashmiri chillies, garlic, and coriander powder, till the onion softens. Add grated coconut. Remove from heat and cool.
3. Grind this mixture to a fine paste along with tomatoes and turmeric and keep aside.
4. In a pan, heat 4 tbsp oil, add fenugreek, mustard seeds, curry leaves, red chilli powder, ginger-garlic paste and the above ground paste, with salt to taste.
5. Keep stirring till it boils. Add 1 glass of water, brinjal, green chillies, and fresh coriander, and leave for 15 minutes on slow fire.

Zulekha Baingan

Spiced Brinjal   *Serves: 4-6*

Ingredients

½ kg	Small thorny brinjal (*gavthi baingan*)
4	Onions (3 sliced and one cut into rings)
½ tsp	Coriander powder (*dhania* powder)
½ tsp	Red chilli powder
2 tsp	Dry Mango (*amchur* powder)

Fresh coriander leaves for garnishing
Salt to taste
Oil for frying

Method

1. Slice the brinjals into two. Make slits on the slices.
2. Put them in salted water for 10 minutes.
3. Remove from salted water and press out all the water with paper or cloth napkins.
4. Deep fry the brinjal slices.
5. Separately, deep fry 3 sliced onions till light brown. Add salt, coriander powder, red chilli powder, dry mango (*amchur*) powder. Mix well.
6. Take the remaining onion, cut into rings, separate the rings. Place on a serving dish.
7. Layer the fried brinjal over the raw onion ring.
8. Then layer the fried onions over the brinjals.
9. Garnish with fresh coriander leaves.
10. Serve.

Chawlai Bhaji

Sautéed cow pea leaves

Serves: 4

Ingredients

2 bunches	Cow pea leaves (green *chawlai*)
2 tbsp	Oil
2	Onions (chopped)
3	Green chillis (chopped)
3	Garlic cloves (chopped)
1 tsp	Ginger-garlic Paste
½ tsp	Turmeric (*haldi* powder)
1 tsp	Coriander (*dhania* powder)
4 tbsp	Grated coconut
Salt to taste	

Method

1. Cut the leaves, wash and keep aside.

2. Heat oil in a pan. Add the onion, green chillies, and garlic and fry for 2 minutes.

3. Then add salt, ginger-garlic paste, turmeric, coriander and stir well.

4. Lastly, add the green *chawlai*, mix well, cover the pan and cook for 10 minutes.

5. Garnish with grated coconut and simmer on slow fire for 10 minutes till cooked.

Aloo Tikki

Mashed potato patties

Ingredients

1 kg	Potatoes
6	Green chillis (chopped)
½ bunch	Fresh coriander
1 tbsp	Dry mango powder (*amchur* powder)
Oil for frying	
Salt to taste	

Method

1. Boil potatoes in a pressure cooker along with water and salt till cooked. This should take around 3 to 4 whistles.

2. Remove from flame, cool, peel and mash the potatoes.

3. Add green chillies, chopped coriander, salt to taste, *amchur* powder and mix well.

4. Form small patties (*tikkis*) of about 1-inch diametre from this mixture.

5. In a frying pan, add enough oil and heat well on medium flame.

6. Deep fry the patties till light brown, and serve.

Aloo Mattar

Dry spiced peas and potatoes

Ingredients

½ kg	Shelled peas (*mattar*)
2 Large	Potatoes (diced)
1	Onion (chopped)
1 tsp	Cumin seeds (*jeera* seeds)
5-6	Curry leaves
1 tbsp	Ginger-garlic paste
1 tsp	Turmeric powder (*haldi* powder)
1 tsp	Coriander powder (*dhania* powder)
2 tsp	Red chilli powder (*lal mirch* powder)
5 Large	Tomatoes (pureed)
2 tbsp	Oil
Salt to taste	

Method

1. Heat oil, add cumin seeds, curry leaves, and onion. Sauté till onions are light brown.

2. Add the ginger-garlic paste, turmeric powder, coriander powder and red chilli powder – mix well.

3. Add the potatoes and peas and cook for 10 minutes.

4. Add the tomato puree and sauté for a few minutes. Then add a glass of water and salt and cook on low flame for 15 minutes.

5. Serve hot.

Bangalori Dal

Flavourful dal made with South Indian spices

Serves: 8

Ingredients

½ cup	Split pigeon pea dal (*tuwar* dal)	2 tsp	Fenugreek seeds (*methi dana*)
½ cup	Split red dal (*masoor* dal)	2 tsp	Cumin powder (*jeera* powder)
2 medium	Tomatoes (chopped)		
2 large	Onions (chopped)	1 cup	Tamarind (*imli*) water
½ bunch	Fresh coriander (*dhania pata* – chopped)	20	Curry leaves
		10	Cloves garlic
4 to 5	Green chillis	3	Dried red chillies (*sabut lal mirch*)
¼	Coconut (ground)		
1 tsp	Red chilli (*lal mirch* powder)	½ tsp	Mustard seeds (*sarson* seeds)
½ tsp	Dry coriander (*dhania* powder)	½ tsp	Asafoetida (*hing*)
		2 tbsp	Oil
¼ tsp	Turmeric (*haldi* powder)	Salt to taste	

Method

1. In a large pan, mix in the *tuwar* dal and *masoor* dal, tomatoes, onion, fresh coriander, green chillies, coconut, red chilli powder, coriander powder, turmeric powder and add enough water to cover all these ingredients.

2. Place the pan on a high flame to cook. You can even use a pressure cooker and cook the dal for at least 5 whistles.

3. When the dal is cooked, mash it into a paste, making sure not to leave any lumps.

4. Stir in the tamarind water.

5. In a separate pan, pour oil. As the oil heats up, add curry leaves, garlic, red chillies, mustard seeds, asafoetida, fenugreek, cumin and sliced onion.

6. Fry this for two to three minutes and quickly pour into the dal mixture, stir and cover so that the aroma is packed in.

7. Serve after 5 minutes.

Dahi ki Curry

Yoghurt curry

Serves: 6

Ingredients

500 gm	Yoghurt (*dahi*)
200 ml	Water
100 gm	Besan
10	Green chillies, chopped
2 tbsp	Ginger, juliennes
5 tbsp	Oil
3	Dried red chillies (*sabut lal mirch*)
1 tsp	Cumin (*jeera*) seeds
1 tsp	Asafoetida (*hing*)
20	Curry leaves
1 bunch	Fresh coriander (*dhania pata*)
Salt to taste	

Method

1. Add water and salt to the yoghurt till it has a buttermilk (*chaach*) consistency.
2. Next add the besan to thicken it along with green chillies and ginger.
3. Let the mixture come to a boil.
4. In a separate pan, heat some oil. Add red chillies, cumin and asafoetida.
5. After 2 minutes, pour this mixture into the yoghurt gravy.
6. Add the curry leaves and boil for 15 minutes on a high flame.
7. Garnish with fresh coriander. Serve.

Dalcha with Dudhi

Hyderabadi stew with bottle gourd

Serves: 6

Step 1		Step 2	
½ kg	Split pigeon pea dal (*tuwar dal*)/ Split red dal (*masoor dal*)	4 tpsp	Oil
		1 tsp	Cumin
		1 tsp	Mustard
1 tsp	Turmeric powder (*haldi powder*)	1	Onion
		5-6	Curry leaves
1 tsp	Red chilli powder	10	Flakes garlic
1 large	Bottle gourd (*dudhi*) cut into pieces.		
Salt to taste			

Put the above ingredients in a cooker with 1 litre water. Cook till 1 whistle. Cool. Open the cooker. Add *dudhi* pieces.

1. Take a pan add 4 tpsp oil, 1 tsp cumin (*jeera*) seeds, 1 tsp mustard (*sarson*) seed, 1 onion cut, 10 flakes garlic cut into small pieces, 8 round red chillies, 5-6 curry leaves, fry till light brown.

2. Add 1 tsp red chilli powder and salt. Add this to the cooker mixture. Simmer till *dudhi* is cooked.

3. Garnish with fresh coriander.

Biryanis Pulaus & Rice

Prawn Pulau
Prawn pilaf

Serves: 8

1 kg	Rice	1 large	Bay leaf (*tej pata*)
2 kg	Prawns (shelled)	6	Cloves (*laung*)
1½ tbsp	Ginger-garlic paste	6	Cardamom (*elaichi*)
½ tsp	Cumin (*jeera*) powder	2 to 3 large	Tomatoes (chopped)
1 tbsp	Coriander (*dhania*) powder	2 large	Potatoes (sliced)
½ bunch	Coriander (*dhania pata*) fresh	2 large	Onions (sliced)
1 tbsp	Red chilli (*lal mirch*) powder	½ tsp	Saffron (*kesar*)
¼ tsp	Turmeric (*haldi*) powder	1	Lime juice
½	Coconut	Salt to taste	
9	Dry red chillies	Oil for frying	

Method

1. Grind together the ginger-garlic paste, cumin, coriander, turmeric powder, coconut, red chillies, cardamom, cloves, and salt to taste.

2. Heat oil, add the bay leaf. Then add the masala and fry well.

3. Add the cleaned prawns with a little water to cook.

4. After the prawns are done, add the tomatoes and cook till all the water evaporates. Keep this prawn masala aside.

5. Fry the potatoes in a separate pan and keep aside.

6. Fry the onions till golden brown.

7. Par-boil the rice.

8. In a separate deep pan make layers of par-boiled rice, prawns, potatoes and end with a layer of onions.

9. Soak some saffron in hot water, or preferably lime juice, and pour over the layered rice.

10. Tightly close the lid and leave on dum till ready to serve.

Kheema Pulau

Mincemeat pilaf

Ingredients

1 kg	Mincemeat (*kheema*)	2 tbsp	Ginger-garlic paste
1 kg	Rice	Salt to taste	
6	Cardamoms (*elaichi*)	10	Green chillies, ground
6	Cloves (*laung*)	4 tbsp	Oil/ 2 tbsp ghee
2 large sticks	Cinnamon (*dalchini*)	½ kg	Tomatoes, chopped
2 large	Onions (finely sliced)	¼ kg	Split red lentil (*masoor* dal)
¾	Whole coconut, grated	½ kg	Yoghurt (*dahi*)
½ bunch	Coriander (*dhania pata*), pureed	2	Lemons, juiced
2 tsp	Red chilli (*lal mirch*) powder	15	Mint (*pudina*) leaves, whole
¾ tsp	Turmeric (*haldi*) powder	2 tsp	Garam masala

Method

1. Heat the oil/ghee in a pan. Add cardamom, cloves, cinnamon and sauté. Add finely sliced onions and fry till light brown.
2. In a bowl, mix the *kheema* with coconut, coriander, red chilli powder, turmeric, ginger-garlic paste, and salt to taste.
3. Put this mixture into the pan with the browned onions and continue frying.
4. Add the tomatoes and fry till the tomatoes are mashed into the *kheema*.
5. Drain both the rice and *masoor* dal and add to the *kheema*.
6. Fry for 10 minutes. Then add the lime juice and yoghurt and mix well.
7. Pour about 10 glasses of water, just enough to cover the rice. Check the seasoning.
8. Add the mint leaves and cover the pan.
9. After 5 minutes open the pan, add green chillies and garam masala.
10. Stir, then cover the pan again and allow the rice to cook till all the water evaporates. leave the pulao on *dum*.
11. Sprinkle some golden brown onions on top of the dish before serving.

Chop Pulau

Pilaf with lamb chops

Serves: 15

2 kg	Rice		2 tsp	Ginger-garlic paste
2 kg	Mutton chops		1½ tsp	Peppercorns (*sabut kali mirch*)
3 tsp	Pepper (*kali mirch*), ground		¼ kg	Butter
4 sticks of 1" each	Cinnamon (*dalchini*)		4 large	Onions, chopped
			10 small	Potatoes, whole with skin
6	Cloves (*laung*)		1 tbsp	Cumin (*jeera*) seeds
8	Cardamoms (*elaichi*)		1 tsp	Garam masala
½ bunch	Fresh coriander (*dhania pata*)		Salt to taste	
15	Green chillies		Oil for frying	

1. Place washed chops in a cooker with ground pepper, cinnamon, cloves, cardamom, 2 glasses water and salt to taste. Cook till tender.

2. In a blender, grind coriander, green chillies, ginger-garlic paste, peppercorns with salt to taste and a little water.

3. In a separate pan add butter and fry chopped onions till light brown. Add cumin.

4. Separately parboil the potatoes with the skin and keep aside.

5. Add ground masala into the onion mixture and fry on a high flame till masala is well-fried and the butter in the pan comes to the top.

6. Add a little water and the parboiled potatoes.

7. Once the potatoes are soft and the masala mixture is a thick green gravy, add the mutton chops from the cooker. Do not add the meat stock. Fry all this together.

8. Once the chops are fried along with the potatoes, add the garam masala.

9. Add the meat stock from the cooker and let it all come to a boil. For 4 cups of rice, add 7½ cups of water and around 1½ cups meat stock.

10. Add the washed and drained rice. Bring to a boil. Then place the rice and meat mixture on slow fire and let it simmer for 45 minutes until the rice is cooked.

11. Serve with a salad of tomato, onion, fresh coriander, green chillies and vinegar.

Fish Pulau

Fish pilaf

Ingredients

500 gms	Fish, cut into large slices	3	Potatoes, cut into round thick slices
1	Coconut milk		
1 kg	Rice	1 tsp	Cumin (*jeera*) seeds
3	Onions, finely chopped	1 bunch	Fresh coriander (*dhania pata*)
4	Cloves (*laung*)	2 tsp	Garlic paste
4	Cardamoms (*elaichi*)	4 tbsp	Oil
1"	Cinnamon (*dalchini*)	Salt to taste	
¾ tsp	Turmeric (*haldi*) powder	Green chillies for garnishing	
2 tsp	Red chilli powder		

Method

1. (In one cup of rice 2 glasses of coconut milk is required).
2. Fry the onions till brown with cloves, cardamoms and cinnamon.
3. Marinate the fish with salt, turmeric, red chilli powder, lemon juice and keep aside for 1 hour. Lightly fry the fish.
4. Deep fry the potatoes and keep aside.
5. Grind cumin, coriander, garlic together. Add the fried onion mixture to this masala and fry together.
6. Now add the coconut milk and let it cook, bringing it to a boil.
7. Then place the fish in the gravy and bring to a boil.
8. Remove the fish and keep aside.
9. Now add the rice to the gravy. Make sure it is immersed in the coconut milk.
10. When the rice is cooked, remove from the fire.
11. In a separate pan, spread a layer of rice at the bottom, then the fried potatoes and repeat.
12. On the last layer spread the fish pieces right on top and add some fresh coriander and slit green chillies and leave on slow fire for 5 more minutes and serve.

Sabzi Gosht Pulau

Vegetable and mutton pilaf

Serves: 8-10

Ingredients

1 kg	Mutton pieces	1 tsp	Coriander (*dhania*) powder
1½ kg	Rice	2 tsp	Red chilli (*lal mirch*) powder
100 gm	Ghee	4	Tomatoes, chopped
2 tbsp	Oil	2 bunch	Spinach (*palak*)
4	Cloves (*laung*)	½ bunch	Dill (*sui*) leaves
4"	Cinnamon (*dalchini*)	½ bunch	Fenugreek (*methi*) leaves
4	Cardamom (*elaichi*)	¼ kg	French beans
3	Onions (chopped)	2	Potatoes, cut into 8 pieces
2 tbsp	Ginger-garlic paste	Salt to taste	
1 tsp	Turmeric (*haldi*) powder		

Method

1. Heat oil in a pan.
2. Add cloves, cinnamon, cardamon, onions, and simmer till light brown.
3. Add ginger-garlic paste.
4. Add mutton and mix well.
5. Add turmeric, coriander, red chilli powder, salt and tomatoes.
6. Keep on medium flame and cook till done.
7. Add spinach, dill, fenugreek leaves, beans, potatoes and cook till tender.
8. Cook rice separately till half done and drain the water.
9. Place the rice over the cooked vegetables and mutton.
10. Heat ghee in a separate pan and pour over the rice.
11. Cook on slow fire for 15 minutes.

Biryani Masala Rice

Pilaf cooked with biryani masalas

Ingredients

1 kg	Rice soaked in water	2	Onions, sliced
6	Cloves (*laung*)	4	Tomatoes, chopped
6	Green cardamom (*choti elaichi*)	½ cup	Yoghurt (*dahi*)
		½ tsp	Turmeric (*haldi*) powder
2 tsp	Ginger-garlic paste	¼ bunch	Mint (*pudina*) leaves
1 bunch	Fresh coriander (*dhania pata*)	5	Green chillies, slit in half
		4 tbsp	Oil
10	Dried red chillies (*sabut lal mirch*)	Salt to taste	

Method

1. Grind cloves, cardamom, ginger-garlic paste, fresh coriander and red chillies together to make a masala.

2. In a pan, fry onions till light brown and then add ground masala from step 1 and fry for a few minutes.

3. Add tomatoes and keep frying till they are mashed in with the rest of the ingredients.

4. Mix in yoghurt with salt to taste and a pinch of turmeric.

5. After the masala is well-browned, drain the soaked rice and fry with the masala in the pan for 5 minutes.

6. Separately boil water (6 cups of water for 1 kg rice) and pour into the pan with the masala and rice.

7. Stir in the mint leaves, coriander, and green chillies.

8. Close the lid and let the rice cook on slow fire till done.

Chicken Biryani Lazeez with Potato

Chicken biryani with cut potatoes

Serves: 15

Ingredients

2 kg	Rice	2 sticks	Cinnamon (*dalchini*)
3	Chickens, whole, cut into pieces	2 tbsp	Ginger-garlic paste
1 cup	Milk	2 tsp	Red chilli (*lal mirchi*) powder
1 cup	Ghee	5	Onions, sliced
3 tbsp	Oil	4	Tomatoes, chopped
6	Potatoes, cut into halves	200 gm	Yoghurt (*dahi*)
10 gm	Mace (*jawitri*)	2	Large lemons, juiced
10 gm	Black cumin seeds (*shahi jeera*)	Pinch	Saffron (*zaffran*)
4	Cardamoms (*elaichi*)	Salt to taste	
4	Cloves (*laung*)		

Method

1. Boil potatoes with salt and keep aside.
2. Grind to a fine paste the mace, black cumin seeds, cinnamon, cardamom, clove, ginger-garlic paste, red chilli powder, and salt to taste.
3. Mix the chicken pieces with yoghurt and marinate.
4. Fry the potatoes lightly and keep aside.
5. In the same pan, fry the onions to a light golden brown.
6. Remove half the onions from the pan and keep aside.
7. Now add the ground masala (step 2) to the onions in the pan, stir well. Fry well till the masala is well-browned.
8. Add the tomatoes, keep frying till the liquid from the tomatoes evaporates.
9. Add the chicken with yoghurt marinade and keep browning on high flame for a further 10 to 15 minutes.
10. Pour the lemon juice into the chicken gravy.

11. The remaining onions should be fried till crisp golden brown, without allowing it to burn. Then cooled and crushed and put it into the chicken gravy.

12. Finally, add the light golden fried potatoes into the chicken.

13. Cook the rice separately in another pan.

14. In another pan, spread the rice at the base, then the chicken gravy and some potatoes.

15. Keep alternating the layers – the top layer should be of rice.

16. Take milk, add 1 tsp sugar, a pinch of saffron and pour over the rice.

17. Pour melted ghee over the rice. Cover with a lid.

18. Take a tawa and place the pan on it.

19. Leave on a slow fire for 10 minutes.

20. Serve with kachumber salad (see page 185).

Mutton Biryani

Mutton pilaf

Ingredients

3 tbsp	Oil	4 large	Potatoes, halved
1 kg	Meat	4	Cardamoms (*elaichi*)
2 tbsp	Garlic-ginger paste	4	Cloves (*laung*)
3 tsp	Red chilli (*lal mirch*) powder	1"	Cinnamon (*dalchini*)
1 tsp	Turmeric (*haldi*) powder	Pinch	Saffron (*zaffran*)
½ kg	Yoghurt (*dahi*)	1 tsp	Milk
1½	Lemons, juiced	1 tsp	Garam masala powder
1½ kg	Onions, sliced	1 kg	Cooked rice
1½ kg	Tomatoes, chopped	Salt to taste	

Method

1. Wash the meat well and marinate it with garlic-ginger paste, red chilli powder, turmeric, yoghurt, lemon juice, salt to taste. Leave the meat to marinate for an hour.

2. In a pan, add oil and fry the sliced onions until light golden brown along with cardamom, cloves and cinnamon for added flavour (do not let the onions become dark brown).

3. When the onions are golden brown, remove from the pan and crush by hand. Put the remaining oil left in the pan into the marinated meat.

4. Add the chopped tomatoes and the crushed onions to the meat. Mix well and put on a high flame till the meat mixture comes to a boil. Then close the lid and leave to simmer for about 45 minutes.

5. Fry the potatoes with salt till golden brown and keep aside.

6. When the meat is cooked, add the fried potatoes (do not pour any water into the meat; allow it to cook in the tomato, yoghurt and meat juices itself).

7. In another pan spread the cooked white rice on the base, then place the meat over it and repeat the layering till all the meat and rice is used.

8. Sprinkle some garam masala and a little bit of saffron mixed in milk over the last layer and cook on slow fire for 15 minutes. To serve the biryani, dig ladle right into the pan and bring out the rice in layers so that the separation is visible on the serving dish.

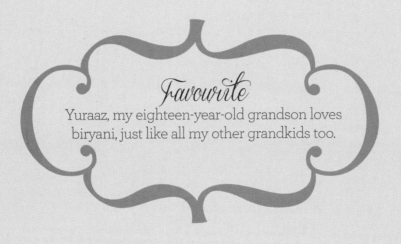

Favourite

Yuraaz, my eighteen-year-old grandson loves
biryani, just like all my other grandkids too.

Khichri

Stewed dal and rice

Serves: 8

Ingredients

½ kg	Rice
250 gm	Split yellow gram (*moong* dal)
2	Onions, sliced
1 tsp	Cumin (*jeera*) seeds
4	Garlic, cloves
1 tsp	Turmeric (*haldi*) powder
4"	Cinnamon (*dalchini*)
4	Green cardamoms (*choti elaichi*)
4	Green chillies
½ bunch	Fresh coriander (*dhaniya pata*)
¼ bunch	Mint (*pudina*) leaves
2 tbsp	Oil
3 tbsp	Ghee
Salt to taste	

Method

1. Soak rice and dal in water for 20 minutes.
2. In a heavy-bottom pan, heat ghee and oil. Add cumin, onion, cloves, cinnamon, cardamom and fry for 5 minutes.
3. Add rice, dal, turmeric, and salt to taste.
4. Add green chillies, fresh coriander, and mint leaves with 1½ glasses of water.
5. Cook for half an hour till the water evaporates.

Brown Rice for Dhansak

Parsi mutton and lentil stew, with brown rice

Serves: 8

Ingredients

1 kg	Rice, soaked in 1 litre water
2 big	Onions, sliced
5	Cloves (*laung*)
5	Cardamoms (*elaichi*)
10 whole	Black peppercorns (*sabut kali mirch*)
6	Cinnamon sticks (*dalchini*)
Oil	4 tbsp
Salt to taste	

Method

1. Fry onions, cloves, cardamom, black pepper, and cinnamon till onions have turned dark brown.

2. Then add the drained rice and stir well.

3. Add 1 litre water and cover the pan with a lid and let it cook.

4. As it comes to a boil, lower the heat and let it simmer till the rice is cooked.

5. Sprinkle onion barista on top (onion fried till browned). You can fry 1 large sliced onion in 3 tbsp oil, till the onion is golden brown. Drain the oil out and use the onions.

6. Serve.

Favourite

My youngest
daughter
Sussanne loves
the chicken korma
and challau made
at home.

Challau Rice

Pilaf flavoured with dried fruits

 Ingredients

½ kg	Rice
2	Onions, sliced
100 gm	Raisins (*kishmish*)
½ tsp	Saffron (*zaffran*)
1 tbsp	Milk
Oil for frying	
Salt to taste	

Method

1. Boil or steam the rice till cooked.

2. Fry the onions till golden brown. Add the raisins and fry till light brown and swollen.

3. Soak the saffron in milk.

4. Place the rice on a serving plate and garnish with fried onions, raisins, and saffron milk. Serve hot.

Fish & other Seafood

Fish Fry in Green Masala-Pomfret

Fish fried with coriander and chilli marinade

Ingredients

3	Pomfrets – whole, small, or medium

For the masala:

½ bunch	Fresh coriander (*dhania pata*)
5	Green chillies
½ tsp	Cumin (*jeera*) seeds
2 tsp	Coconut powder
1	Lime juice
5 Flakes	Garlic
10 whole	Black peppercorns (*sabut kali mirch*)
Salt to taste	
Oil for frying	

Method

1. Clean and wash the pomfret.
2. Grind all the ingredients for the masala.
3. Make a few cuts on the fish and apply the ground masala.
4. Let this marinate for at least half an hour.
5. Fry the fish, and just before serving, squeeze lime over it.

Fish /Prawn Patia

Spicy dry seafood delicacy

Serves: 6

Ingredients

2	Pomfret, sliced or 1 kg prawns	2 tsp	Sugar
1 tsp	Turmeric (*haldi*) powder	3 tbsp	Coriander (*dhania*) powder
1 tsp	Cumin (*jeera*) powder	4 large	Tomatoes
10 flakes	Garlic	5	Green chillies, slit
10 dried	Red chillies	2 tbsp	Oil
2 large	Onions	Chopped coriander for garnish	
4 tbsp	Vinegar	Salt to taste	

Method

1. Clean the fish/prawns and keep aside.

2. Grind turmeric, cumin, and garlic together.

3. Marinate the fish/prawns in this mixture and keep aside.

4. Mix red chillies with a little bit of water to make into a paste. Set aside.

5. Heat oil in a separate pan and sauté onions till light brown.

6. Add chilli paste along with vinegar, sugar, ground coriander, and chopped tomatoes. If desired, add water for extra gravy.

7. Stir continuously and cook this mixture well on a slow fire till the tomatoes are mashed and mixed well with the onions.

8. Now add the marinated fish/prawns and bring to a boil for 3 minutes. Lower the heat and add salt to taste.

9. Lastly add green chillies, finely chopped coriander, and cook on slow fire for 5 minutes till the oil comes on top.

White Fish Curry

Fish in white gravy

Ingredients

2 big	Pomfrets, cut into pieces
4 tsp	Rice, uncooked
1	Coconut, grated
2 tsp	Garlic-ginger paste
5 to 6	Green chillies, slit
1 tsp	Cumin (*jeera*), seeds
7 to 8 small	Tomatoes
½ cup	White vinegar
3 tbsp	Oil
Fresh coriander	
Salt to taste	

Method

1. Take uncooked rice and put on a griddle (*tawa*) to heat a bit, then put in the blender and grind into a fine paste by adding a little water.

2. Mix the rice paste and the grated coconut together and add some more water so as to extract 2 glasses of coconut milk from this, and keep aside.

3. Heat oil in a pan and add garlic-ginger paste; 2 minutes later, add cut chillies and cumin.

4. After 2-3 minutes, add the coconut mixture into the pan and let it boil on very slow fire.

5. Keep stirring occasionally for 30 minutes or so till the gravy thickens.

6. Add tomatoes and fish slices.

7. Stir in the white vinegar.

8. When the fish is cooked, in approximately 15 to 20 minutes, sprinkle fresh coriander and 4 to 5 half-slit green chillies and leave to cook on slow fire for 5 minutes.

9. Serve.

Red Masala Prawns/Fried Pomfret

Fried prawn/fish with a red marinade

Serves: 4-6

Ingredients

1 kg	Prawns or 1 Pomfret, sliced
1 tsp	Ginger paste
2 tsp	Garlic paste
3 tsp	Red chilli (*lal mirch*) powder
½ tsp	Turmeric (*haldi*) powder
1 tsp	Coriander (*dhania*) powder
1	Lemon, juiced
Oil for frying	
Salt to taste	

Method

1. Wash the prawns/fish and cut into slices.
2. Grind together ginger paste, garlic paste, red chilli powder, coriander powder, turmeric and salt.
3. Add the lime juice to this masala. Apply the masala on the prawns/fish.
4. Marinate for an hour and then fry the prawns/fish in oil for 15 minutes till cooked.

Hyderabadi Prawn Curry

Spicy prawn curry

Serves: 6-8

1 kg	Large prawns	1 tbsp	Coriander (*dhania*) powder
4 tbsp	Oil	1 tbsp	Red chilli (*lal mirch*) powder
1 kg	Tomatoes	9 to 10	Garlic, cloves
1 tsp	Cumin (*jeera*) powder	9 to 10	Dry red chillies
1 tsp	Turmeric (*haldi*) powder	10	Curry leaves
½ tsp	Fenugreek (*methi*) seeds	Salt to taste	

1. Boil tomatoes in water and remove the skin, puree in a food processor.
2. Heat oil in a pan and add cumin, fenugreek seeds, coriander powder, and red chilli powder. Fry for 3 minutes.
3. Add the garlic, red chillies, and curry leaves. Fry for a few minutes.
4. Then add the tomato puree and continue frying.
5. Add salt to taste.
6. Reduce heat and let simmer till the oil rises to the top of the pan.
7. Now add the cleaned and dried prawns (make sure the prawns are completely dry). Usually prawns curl in around 8 to 10 minutes. If the prawns have released too much water, remove the prawns from the pan (or else the prawns will turn hard) and let the excess water evaporate on high fire. Once the gravy has become the consistency that you require, put the prawns back in the pan (this curry must not be too watery and more like a thick paste).
8. Even when reheating, remove the prawns from the gravy. This will ensure the prawns remain soft. Mix the prawns in once the gravy is heated.
9. Serve with rice.

Prawn Kebabs

Kebabs made with minced prawns

Serves: 8

Ingredients

1 kg	Prawns
6	Green chillies
½ bunch	Fresh coriander (*dhania pata*)
1 pod	Garlic
1 tsp	Cumin (*jeera*) seeds
1 tsp	Turmeric (*haldi*) powder
1	Onion, cut into rings
½ cup	Mint (*pudina*) leaves
2	Lemons, juiced

Bread crumbs
Oil for frying
Salt to taste

Method

1. Grind together green chillies, coriander, garlic, cumin, and salt to taste.
2. Take the cleaned prawns and mix with ground masala (step 1), turmeric powder and grind in the mixer.
3. Take the mixture and form tiny round balls or cutlet shaped pieces.
4. Coat with bread crumbs and deep fry.
5. Once fried, sprinkle with lemon juice and garnish with onion rings and mint leaves. Serve instantly.

Patra Ni Macchi

Fish Steamed in Banana Leaves

Ingredients

2	Pomfret, cut into pieces	1 tbsp	Cumin (*jeera*) seeds
1	Coconut, grated	2 tbsp	Sugar
2 bunches	Fresh coriander (*dhania*	2	Lemons, juiced
	pata), finely chopped	1 tbsp	Vinegar
¼ cup	Mint leaves (*pudina*)	10 to 12	Curry leaves
1 piece (medium)	Ginger	Banana leaves - as required to cover the
20	Garlic cloves		fish pieces
8	Cloves (*laung*)	2 tbsp	Oil
10	Green chillies, deseeded	Salt to taste	
10	Peppercorns (*kali mirch*)		

Method

1. Wash the pomfret well, cut into large pieces and set aside.
2. Grind the masala for chutney which includes grated coconut, coriander, mint, ginger, garlic, cloves, green chillies, peppercorns, cumin, sugar, and salt to taste. Add lemon juice to the mixture.
3. Prepare the banana leaves by first removing the stalk. Clean and wash them, and then cut into large pieces.
4. Take one piece of fish at a time and make tiny incisions on it with a knife.
5. Coat each piece of fish well with the chutney and leave to marinate for at least 30 minutes.
6. Grease each banana leaf piece lightly with oil. Wrap a piece of fish in it.
7. Wrap the fish pieces in separate leaves. Secure the parcel by tying it with a thin thread.
8. After all the pieces have been neatly wrapped in the banana leaves, take an aluminum tray and grease it well with oil.
9. Arrange the parcels on a tray. Place the tray on medium flame. Cook each side for approximately 3 to 4 minutes.
10. Next sprinkle water, vinegar, and curry leaves on the parcels, cover the dish and allow the fish to steam by placing it in a pan of water on a high stand.
11. Leave this on low flame and cook each side of the parcels for 7 to 8 minutes. Serve instantly.

Parsi Fish/Prawn Sauce

Fish/prawn cooked in white sauce

Serves: 4-6

Ingredients

2	Pomfrets, sliced/ 1 kg prawns	2	Eggs
1 whole pod	Garlic	2 tsp	Sugar
1 tsp	Cumin (*jeera*) seeds	½ cup	Vinegar
6 to 7 half	Green chillies, slit	¼ bunch	Fresh coriander (*dhaniya*)
1 tbsp	Flour (*maida*)	3 tbsp	Oil
8-10	Tomatoes, small	Salt to taste	

Method

1. Heat oil in a pan, add chopped garlic, cumin seeds oil, and green chillies.

2. Fry this for 2 minutes. Add flour with a glass of water and keep stirring till it becomes a fine paste.

3. Add water, salt, tomatoes and allow to boil.

4. Add the fish/prawns (if fish, then leave it on for 5 minutes till it is semi done). If prawns then let it cook for 15 to 20 minutes till done.

5. Remove pan from heat and allow it to cool completely.

6. In a separate bowl, whisk the eggs, mix in sugar and vinegar.

7. When the sugar has dissolved completely, add this mixture to the cooled fish/prawns.

8. Put back onto the fire and keep stirring continuously till the sauce thickens to the derived consistency.

9. Top this with cut fresh coriander and serve with yellow rice or *khichri* (pg 68).

   (If you are making fish sauce, first remove the fish pieces from the pan before stirring or else the fish pieces will flake and break).

Mummy's Style Fish Curry

Tangy fish curry

Serves: 4-6

2 large	Pomfret	**For the ground masala:**	
1 tsp	Turmeric (*haldi*) powder	1 tsp	Cumin (*jeera*) seeds
2	Onions, finely chopped	½ tsp	Fenugreek (*methi*) seeds
1 large	Tomato, finely chopped	2 tsp	Red chilli (*lal mirch*) powder
1 tbsp	Tamarind (*imli*) water	1 tsp	Coriander (*dhania*) powder
5 to 6	Green chillies, slit	½ tsp	Turmeric (*haldi*)
200 ml	Coconut milk	1	Coconut
Salt to taste		¼ bunch	Fresh coriander (*dhania pata*)
4 tbsp	Oil		

1. Wash the fish well.
2. Add turmeric and salt to the fish. Shallow-fry the fish and keep aside.
3. Fry the finely chopped onions in another pan till light brown.
4. Add the ground masala to the onions and cook till mixed well.
5. Add the tomato and keep frying till it has cooked through.
6. Add the tamarind water and then mix in as much water as required for a gravy. You could also add 200 ml of coconut milk. (Preferably use only coconut milk.)
7. Bring to a boil. Add the fish and simmer for 10 to 15 minutes till the fish is cooked.
8. Lastly, sprinkle some fresh coriander and slit green chillies and leave on a low flame till you see a thin layer of oil on the top of the gravy.
9. Serve with rice.

Maida Fish Fry

Fish fried in flour batter

Serves: 2-3

Ingredients

2 to 3 medium	Pomfrets (whole)
6 small	Garlic, cloves
½ tsp	Carom (*ajwain*) seeds
3	Green chillies
½ bunch	Fresh coriander
1 tbsp	Coriander seeds (*dhania*)
½ tsp	Garam masala
2 tbsp	Gram flour (*besan*)
1 tsp	Flour (*maida*)
1 tsp	Lemon juice
Oil for frying	
Salt to taste	

Method

1. Grind together the garlic, carom seeds, green chillies, fresh coriander, coriander seeds, garam masala and salt to taste.

2. Spread this over the fish, leave to marinate for ½ hour.

3. Mix besan and flour with a little water to make a paste.

4. Rub this all over the fish.

5. Shallow fry the fish till half cooked.

6. When ready to serve, fry the fish till it is cooked through.

7. Squeeze lemon juice over the fish before serving.

Spicy Green Mango Prawn Curry

Ingredients

4 to 5 medium	Green Mangoes	8	Cloves garlic
25 to 30	Prawns, large	1 small piece	Ginger
10	Kashmiri chillies	¾ tsp	Turmeric
8	Full Black Pepper Corns	1	Whole Coconut
2 tsp	Coriander seeds	12	Curry leaves
1 tsp	Sesame seeds	1 bunch	Fresh coriander
1 tsp	Asafoetida (*Hing*)	Salt to taste	
1	Onion, finely sliced	2 tbsp	Oil

Method

1. Peel and cut green mangoes. Do not remove the inside stone. Wash and keep aside.

2. Take prawns and clean well by removing the black vien.

3. Boil together the mango and the prawns with salt to taste and keep aside.

4. Take kashmiri chillies, full black pepper corns, coriander seeds, sesame seeds, hing, onion, garlic, ginger, turmeric, and coconut and grind all this together.

5. Heat oil in a separate pan and fry curry leaves, and then add the ground masala and fry all together well till oil comes on the top.

6. Then add 4 to 5 cups of water in the same pan and let it simmer for 4 to 5 minutes on high flame and then slow the flame and add salt to taste.

7. When this comes to a boil, add the prawns and the mangoes only and sprinkle fresh coriander and let it simmer on slow fire for 5 more minutes till the oil comes on top.

8. Serve with rice.

Surmai Fry

Boneless fish fry   *Serves: 6-8*

Ingredients

1 Medium	Surmai (you could also use any other boneless sea fish)
1 tbsp	Chilli (*lal mirch*) powder
2 tbsp	Coriander (*dhania*) powder
1 tsp	Turmeric (*haldi*) powder
1 tbsp	Garlic paste
3 tbsp	Vinegar
1 Lemon	Juiced
Salt to taste	
Oil for frying	

Method

1. Cut and wash the Surmai.
2. Mix red chilli powder, coriander powder, turmeric powder, garlic paste, vinegar, lime juice and salt to taste. Marinate the fish in this paste for half an hour.
3. Shallow fry till light brown.

Crab Curry

Spicy crab curry

Serves: 2-3

Ingredients

6	Crabs	
1½	Coconut	
4 tbsp	Oil	
3	Tomatoes	
2 tbsp	Ginger-garlic paste	
10 whole	Black Peppercorns (*sabut kali mirch*)	
4	Onions, chopped	

For the Garam Masala:

4	Cardamom (*elaichi*)
4	Cloves (*laung*)
1"	Cinnamon/ Dalchini
1 tsp	Cumin (*jeera*)
10	Curry leaves
1 tbsp	Red chilli (*lal mirch*) powder
½ tsp	Turmeric (*haldi*) powder
¼ bunch	Coriander (dried red)
6	chillies deseeded, fried
1	Lemon, juiced
Salt to taste	

Method

1. Grind the coconut along with ginger-garlic paste and peppercorns.
2. In another pan, heat the oil and sauté the garam masala.
3. When it stops spluttering, add curry leaves along with the chopped onions. Fry till light brown.
4. Add the coconut paste and chilli powder, turmeric, tomatoes, salt to taste and fry well.
5. Add one glass water to the paste along with the cracked crabs.
6. Simmer till the crabs are cooked. (The crabs can be steamed earlier in a pressure cooker for 2 or 3 whistles and then put into the curry.)
7. When the dish is ready, garnish with fresh coriander, fried dry red chillies and the lemon juice.
8. Leave it to cook on slow fire for 5 minutes till the oil surfaces. Serve with rice.

Chicken

Baked Chicken

Chicken baked in a spiced white sauce

Ingredients

1 kg	Chicken	2	Green chillies, chopped five
1 tbsp	Ginger-garlic paste	1 tsp	Ground pepper (*kali mirch*)
250 ml	Milk	1	Lemon, juiced
100 gm	Butter	200 gm	Grated cheese
150 gm	Flour (*maida*)	1	Egg
½ bunch	Fresh coriander	Salt to taste	

Method

1. Boil the chicken pieces, along with ginger-garlic paste and salt in two glasses of water.

2. Cover the pan and let the chicken pieces boil on high flame till cooked and the water in the pan is reduced to half.

3. Remove the chicken pieces, cool and shred the chicken off the bones into one-inch pieces. Place the shredded chicken on a flat baking dish. Keep the chicken stock.

4. Add milk, butter, and flour to the chicken stock. Place the pan back on high flame and keep stirring so that no lumps form.

5. Stir till it becomes a semi-thick white sauce with a smooth consistency.

6. Take the baking dish in which you have spread the shredded chicken and cover the chicken with coriander, green chillies, ground pepper, and lemon juice.

7. Pour the white sauce over the chicken mixture.

8. Sprinkle cheese over this and add a little salt to taste.

9. Beat egg and pour over the cheese.

10. Place the baking dish in the oven, and bake at 100 degrees for 45 minutes. Keep checking, and if you see it turning brown, lower the heat accordingly till done.

Chicken Hasina in Black Pepper

Dry pan roasted chicken with black pepper

Serves: 8-10

Ingredients

2 whole	Chicken, cut into pieces
3	Tomatoes, chopped
2 tsp	Red chilli (*lal mirch*) powder
1 tsp	Turmeric (*haldi*) powder
2 tbsp	Ginger-garlic paste
4 tbsp	Oil
2 tsp	Black peppercorn (*kali mirch*)
½ cup	Curry leaves
¼ bunch	Fresh coriander
6 to 8	Green chillies
Salt to taste	

Method

1. Place the chicken and tomatoes in a pan.
2. Add red chilli powder, turmeric, ginger-garlic paste, and salt to taste.
3. Make sure the chicken is well-coated in the paste. Add half a glass of water.
4. Place the pan on high flame for 5 minutes. Then lower the flame and simmer till the chicken is tender.
5. All the liquid from the pan should have evaporated.
6. If need be, place the pan back on a high flame with the lid off to quicken the evaporation process.
7. In a separate pan, heat oil and shallow-fry the chicken pieces.
8. When it is well-browned, add the pepper and fry for another 5 minutes.
9. Lastly, add a few curry leaves, coriander, and green chillies and keep on the flame for 5 minutes. Serve hot.

You can use mutton or lamb instead of chicken. Simply put the meat pieces in a pressure cooker first and follow the same recipe.

Chicken Korma

Mughlai-style chicken in a coconut gravy

Serves: 8-10

2	Chickens	1 tsp	Coriander (*dhania*) powder
2 tbsp	Oil	¼ kg	Yoghurt (*dahi*), whipped
3 large	Onions, chopped	¼ bunch	Fresh coriander (*dhania pata*)
2 tsp	Garlic paste	6 to 8	Green Chillies (slit in half)
2 tsp	Ginger paste	1	Lemon
4 medium	Tomatoes, chopped	1 tbsp	Coconut Powder/ Grated
2 tsp	Red chilli (*lal mirch*) powder		Coconut
½ tsp	Turmeric (*haldi*) powder	Salt to taste	

1. Heat oil in a pan. Add onions, garlic, and ginger paste and fry till well-browned.

2. Remove the mixture and grind into a paste. Keep aside.

3. In the same oil, add tomatoes, fry along with red chilli powder, turmeric powder, coriander powder, and salt to taste.

4. After the tomatoes get fully mashed in the oil, add beaten yoghurt.

5. Pour in the onion paste and keep frying. When this mixture is well-browned, add the chicken and fry for 10 minutes.

6. Add the coconut powder or grated coconut and stir well for at least 5 minutes.

7. Then add ½ glass of water, close the lid and let it simmer on slow fire till the chicken is tender.

8. Add coriander and green chillies and leave on slow flame till the oil rises to the top.

9. Squeeze the juice of the lemon and serve with rice.

Dahi Murg

Chicken cooked with yoghurt

Serves: 8

Ingredients

2	Chickens, cut into medium-size pieces
2 large	Onions, finely chopped
2	Tomatoes, chopped
½ kg	Yoghurt (*dahi*)
¼ tsp	Turmeric (*haldi*) powder
1 tsp	Red chilli (*lal mirch*) powder
2 tbsp	Oil
3	Cardamoms (*elaichi*)
3	Cloves (*laung*)
1 stick	Cinnamon (*dalchini*)
8	Black peppercorns (*kali mirch*)
4	Dried red chillies (*sookhi lal mirch*)
¼ bunch	Fresh coriander (*dhania pata*)
6	Green chillies
Salt to taste	

Method

1. Whip the yoghurt.
2. Add salt, turmeric powder, red chilli powder, chopped onions, chopped tomatoes and chicken. Marinate the chicken in this mixtuire for an hour.
3. In another pan, heat oil. Add cardamom, cloves, cinnamon and black pepper and 2 dried whole red chillies.
4. After 1 minute, add the marinated chicken and curd mixture.
5. Cook on a high flame, then lower to medium till the chicken is tender and the oil surfaces.
6. Sprinkle fresh coriander and slit green chillies and leave on slow fire for 5 minutes.
7. Serve with tomato rice.

Murg Malai Korma

Chicken in a rich yoghurt and cream gravy

Serves: 6

Ingredients

1 kg	Chicken, boneless and cut into medium-sized pieces
3	Tomatoes, chopped
3 tbsp	Oil
2 cups	Yoghurt (*dahi*)
2 tbsp	Ginger-garlic paste
4	Green chillies
1 tsp	Coriander (*dhania*) powder
1 tsp	Cumin (*jeera*) powder
8	Black peppercorns (*sabut kali mirch*), ground
3	Cardamoms (*elaichi*), ground
3	Cloves (*laung*), ground
10	Almonds, ground
150 ml	Fresh cream
¼ bunch	Fresh coriander (*dhania pata*)
Salt to taste	

Method

1. Blend yoghurt, ginger-garlic paste, green chillies, skinned and chopped tomatoes. Keep aside.

2. Heat oil in a pan, add the yoghurt mixture and stir briskly and bring to a boil. Add the chicken pieces.

3. After the chicken gets tender, add coriander, cumin, black peppercorns, cardamom, cloves, and almonds. Fry till the chicken is well coated.

4. Add fresh cream and mix gently.

5. Garnish with coriander while on slow fire and then serve.

Dahi Chicken Barbecue

Yoghurt marinated barbecued chicken

Ingredients

2	Chickens, cut into pieces
1 kg	Yoghurt
3 tbsp	Black pepper (*kali mirch*) powder
2 tbsp	Garlic paste
1	Lemon, juiced
Salt to taste	

Method

1. Marinate the chicken in yoghurt, black pepper, salt, and garlic paste for 2 hours.
2. Heat the coal in the barbecue and place the chicken pieces on it till light brown.
3. Turn the pieces occasionally.
4. Once done, squeeze lemon juice on the pieces, add extra crushed black pepper on the chicken and serve hot with naan.

Chicken Green Masala

Chicken in a coriander gravy   *Serves: 8-10*

2	Chickens, cut into pieces
3	Onions, finely chopped
6	Green chillies
¼ bunch	Fresh coriander (*dhania pata*)
8 to 10	Black Peppercorns (*sabut kali mirch*)
5	Cardamoms (*elaichi*)
6	Cloves (*laung*)
2"	Cinnamon (*dalchini*)
2 tbsp	Ginger-garlic paste
1 tbsp	Coriander (*dhania*) powder
1	Lemon, juiced
2 tbsp	Oil
Salt to taste	

1. Grind onions, green chillies, coriander leaves, black pepper, and salt keep aside.

2. Fry the chicken with cardamom, cloves, and cinnamon till slightly browned.

3. Add the masala paste (step 1), ginger-garlic paste and coriander powder.

4. Keep frying till the masala is cooked, and then add some water for the chicken to cook in.

5. Close the lid and leave on high flame till done. Lower the heat for 5 minutes till the oil rises to the top.

6. Add the lime juice and serve.

Karai Chicken

Chicken in a spicy thick gravy

Serves: 6-8

Ingredients

2	Chickens, cut into pieces
2 tbsp	Oil
6	Green chillies
½ tsp	Turmeric (*haldi*) powder
2 large	Onions, chopped
2 tbsp	Ginger-garlic paste
2 tsp	Red chilli (*lal mirch*) powder
¼ bunch	Fresh coriander (*dhania pata*) leaves
Salt to taste	

Method

1. Heat oil and fry the chicken pieces for 5 minutes.
2. Add green chillies and turmeric and fry for 2 more minutes.
3. Now add just enough water for the chicken to cook and become tender.
4. In another pan, heat oil and fry the onions till light brown. Then add the ginger-garlic paste, salt, and red chilli powder and fry for 5 minutes.
5. Add 2 to 3 tablespoons of water to this onion mixture, cover and allow to simmer on slow fire for a few minutes.
6. Add the fried chicken into this pan and cook on low fire for 5 to 10 minutes. Garnish with coriander and serve.

Note: This is a dry dish. If you would like a bit of gravy, add water accordingly.

Chicken Liver

Sautéed spiced chicken liver

Serves: 8

2 dozen	Chicken livers, chopped into medium-sized pieces
2 large	Onions
3	Green chillies
1 tsp	Ginger paste
1 tsp	Garlic paste
½ tsp	Cumin (*jeera*) powder
1 tsp	Worcestershire sauce
¼ bunch	Fresh coriander (*dhania pata*)
6 to 8 half slit	Green chillies
1	Lemon, juiced
2 tbsp	Oil
Salt to taste	

1. Grind together one onion, green chillies, ginger-garlic, cumin, salt and keep aside.
2. In a pan sauté the other onion (finely chopped) till light brown. Then add the ground masala (step 1) and fry together.
3. Next, add the chicken liver pieces along with Worcestershire sauce and fry.
4. Add just enough water for the liver to cook and become tender along with required salt.
5. Keep on a low flame, stirring occasionally.
6. When ready, add coriander, slit green chillies and the lemon juice and leave on low flame for 5 minutes and serve.

Red Masala Fry Chicken

Chicken fried with a red marinade

Serves: 8-10

Ingredients

2	Chickens, cut into pieces
3 to 4	Cardamoms (*elaichi*)
3 to 4	Cloves (*laung*)
2"	Cinnamon (*dalchini*)
10	Black peppercorns (*sabut kali mirch*, freshly ground)
1½ tbsp	Ginger-garlic paste
3 tbsp	Red chilli (*lal mirch*) powder
1	Lemon, juiced
3 to 4 tbsp	Oil
Salt to taste	

Method

1. Boil chicken pieces in minimum water with cardamom, cloves, cinnamon, whole black pepper, ginger-garlic paste, and salt to taste so that the chicken is almost dry and tender (Do not pressure cook).

2. Remove the chicken pieces from the water (discard the water).

3. Marinate the chicken with red chilli powder, lemon juice, and black pepper for an hour.

4. Take a frying pan and add just enough oil to cover the base. Fry the chicken pieces on a medium flame till they are reddish brown on all sides.

5. Serve immediately.

Sali Chicken

Chicken with potato sticks

Serves: 6-8

1	Chicken, chopped into pieces		3 to 4	Dried red chillies (*sabut lal mirch*)
4	Onions, sliced		1½ tsp	Coriander (*dhania*) powder
3 large	Potatoes, julienned and fried golden brown		1½ tsp	Cumin (*jeera*) powder
			1½ tsp	Red chilli (*lal mirch*) powder
2	Cardamoms (*elaichi*)		½ tsp	Turmeric (*haldi*) powder
2	Cloves (*laung*)		2 tsp	Ginger-garlic paste
10	Black peppercorns (*kali mirch*)		2 tbsp	Oil
3"	Cinnamon (*dal chini*)		Salt to taste	

Method

1. Fry the sliced onions along with the cardamom, cloves, pepper, and cinnamon till the onions are light brown.

2. Add the dried red chillies, coriander, cumin powder, red chilli powder, turmeric and keep frying.

3. Meanwhile, marinate the chicken in ginger-garlic paste and salt.

4. Once the masala in the pan is well-fried, add the chicken to it and keep frying till the chicken browns.

5. Then pour a glass of water into the pan, stir and cover. Lower the flame and simmer till the chicken becomes tender.

6. If you require more gravy, add some water and let it simmer.

7. When serving, garnish with fried julienned potato sticks, also called *sali**, and serve hot.

* (Deep-fry julienned potatoes till light brown without adding any salt.)

Greek Chicken Stifado

Stew flavoured with baby onions

Serves: 10

2	Chickens, cut into pieces
½ kg	Baby onions
5	Tomatoes, boiled, skinned, and mashed into paste
3 tbsp	Tomato sauce
1 tsp	Pepper
1 tsp	Garam Masala
3 tbsp	Oil
Salt to taste	

Method

1. Fry the baby onions till light brown and keep aside.
2. In the same oil, add the chicken pieces and fry till well-browned.
3. Add the tomato paste along with tomato sauce, a little water, salt, and pepper to taste and garam masala powder.
4. When the chicken is half cooked, add the fried baby onions in it and cook together till done.

Palak Chicken

Chicken cooked in spinach

Serves: 10-12

Ingredients

3 medium	Chickens, cut into pieces	1"	Cinnamon (*dalchini*)
3 bunches	Spinach (*palak*)	4	Green chillies
1 bundle	Green fenugreek (*methi*) leaves	2 tsp	Garlic-ginger paste
1 bundles	Dill (*sui bhaji*)	1 tsp	Red chilli (*lal mirch*) powder
3	Onions, finely sliced	½ tsp	Turmeric (*haldi*) powder
4	Tomatoes, chopped	1	Lemon, juiced
3 tbsp	Oil	½ tsp	Garam masala powder
4	Cloves (*laung*)	Salt to taste	
4 whole	Cardamoms (*elaichi*)		

Method

1. Wash and cut the spinach, fenugreek and dill very finely and leave in water for a while. Drain the water.

2. Lightly fry the onion. Add cloves, cardamom, cinnamon, finely-cut green chillies, garlic-ginger paste and fry.

3. Stir in the red chilli powder, turmeric and chicken pieces.

4. Next, add tomatoes and fry together.

5. Once the chicken is fried, add the greens and fry on a high flame.

6. When oil is visible on top of the chicken, add salt to taste and lemon juice. Before serving, sprinkle the garam masala powder.

Egg Curry

Spicy egg gravy

Serves: 8-10

12	Boiled eggs, shelled
1 large	Onion, finely chopped
½ kg	Tomato puree
½ tsp	Cumin (*jeera*) seeds
10 to 20	Curry leaves
1 tbsp	Ginger-garlic paste
1 tsp	Turmeric (*haldi*) powder
2 tsp	Coriander (*dhania*) powder
2 tsp	Red chilli (*lal mirch*) powder
¼ bunch	Coriander (*dhania pata*) leaves
6	Green chillies
Salt to taste	
2 tbsp	Oil

1. Heat oil in a pan.
2. Fry cumin, curry leaves, onion and simmer till light brown.
3. Add ginger-garlic paste, turmeric powder, coriander powder, red chilli powder and tomato puree. Stir and simmer till the oil rises to the top.
4. Add boiled eggs into the tomato gravy.
5. Add coriander, green chillies and cook on slow fire for 10 minutes.
6. Serve with paratha or rice.

Chicken Masala Kashmiri

Serves: 6

1 large	Chicken	10 cloves	Garlic, chopped
10-15	Dried red chillies (*sabut lal mirch*)	½ kg	Yoghurt (*dahi*)
		¼ bunch	Fresh coriander leaves
3 tbsp	Oil	6	Boiled eggs, cut into half
1 tbsp	Ghee	2 large	Potatoes, made into chips
4 large	Onions, chopped	Salt to taste	

Method

1. Boil the Kashmiri chillies. Keep discarding the water and adding fresh water till the chilli water turns a rich red and the chillies are soft.
2. Keep the water aside.
3. In a separate pan, heat ghee and fry the whole chicken till light brown. Remove the chicken from the pan.
4. In the same pan, add the onions and garlic and fry till light brown.
5. Remove from the pan and grind the onions and garlic together.
6. Beat the yoghurt and add it the same pan. Mix the ground onion mixture into the yoghurt and fry for a few minutes.
7. When you see the ghee rising to the top of the yoghurt mixture, pour the red chilli water and keep on high fire.
8. Add 2 to 3 cups of water and bring to a boil.
9. Then put the chicken back into the pan and lower the flame.
10. Let the chicken simmer in this till cooked.
11. Turn it occasionally so that all sides become tender.
12. When the chicken becomes tender and the water from the pan has evaporated, keep frying the chicken in its own fat till the gravy thickens.
13. Sprinkle with coriander and leave to cook on slow fire for 3 minutes.
14. Serve this on a flat dish and garnish with half boiled eggs and potato chips around the chicken.

Chicken Lasagna

Italian baked chicken and pasta

Ingredients

1 kg	Chicken, mince	**Ingredients for White Sauce:**	
2 tbsp	Oil	200 gm	Flour
2	Onions, chopped	1 glass	Milk
4 cloves	Garlic	100 gm	Butter
1 tsp	Pepper (*kali mirch*) powder	100 gm	Mozzarella
2	Tomatoes, chopped	100 gm	Parmesan
4 sheets	Lasagna	250 gm	Processed Cheddar cheese
350 gms	Grated cheese	Salt to taste	

Method

1. First prepare the white sauce, by placing all the ingredients for the sauce in a pan on a low flame and stirring till the sauce thickens.
2. In another pan heat oil and sauté the onions till light brown.
3. Add the mince chicken with garlic, salt and pepper to taste and fry till the chicken is browned and the water has evaporated from the mince.
4. Then add the tomatoes and allow the mince to cook in this till tender.
5. If required, add some water.
6. Fill another large pan with water and bring to a boil. Place the lasagna sheets in it.
7. Cook this on high flame for about 5 minutes till the lasagna sheets rise to the top.
8. Remove the pieces and place on damp cloth.
9. Rub butter on the base of an oblong baking dish, and place a lasagna sheet on it.
10. Cover this with a layer of chicken mince and spread a layer of cheese over this.
11. Cover this with white sauce.
12. Repeat this process ending with a topmost layer of white sauce.
13. Finally, sprinkle cheese on top (preferably Parmesan) and bake for 30 minutes in a preheated (180 degrees) oven.

Bhindi Gosht

Lamb with lady fingers/okra

Serves: 8-10

Ingredients

1 kg	Okra/ Ladyfinger (*bhindi*), chopped
1 kg	Lamb
3 tbsp	Oil
3	Onions, chopped
2 tsp	Ginger-garlic paste
2 tsp	Red chilli (*lal mirch*) powder
1 tsp	Coriander (*dhania*) powder
½ tsp	Turmeric (*haldi*) powder
1 kg	Tomatoes, chopped
1/8th cup	Dry coconut, roughly ground (optional)
5	Green chillies
¼ bunch	Fresh coriander (*dhania pata*)
Salt to taste	

Method

1. Fry onions till light brown. Then add meat pieces with ginger-garlic paste, red chilli powder, coriander powder, turmeric powder, salt to taste, and fry together till well browned.

2. Add the tomatoes along with ground coconut and fry till the tomatoes are well blended with the rest.

3. Then put in the okra and after 2 or 3 minutes of frying, add 1 cup water and cook on medium flame till the water evaporates and the meat is tender.

4. Garnish with green chillies and fresh coriander and serve.

Favourite
Sanjay Khan, my husband,
loves the Persian *aash maash*.

Persian Aash Maash

Persian greens and mince stew

Serves: 8

Ingredients

1 kg	Mince lamb meat (*kheema*)	1 tbsp	Ginger paste
2 cups	Rice	1 big bunch	Dill (*sui bhaji*)
6 tbsp	Ghee	2 kgs beaten	Yoghurt (*dahi*)
1 cup	Yellow Split Pea Lentils (*channa dal*)	3 tbsp	Coarsely ground whole black peppercorns (*sabut kali mirch*)
1 tsp	Turmeric (*haldi*) powder		
2 big bunches	Spring onions (*harra pyaaz*), chopped	12	Green chillies, chopped
		1 small bunch	Mint (*pudina*) leaves
2 tbsp	Garlic paste	Salt to taste	

Method

1. Pressure cook the rice and lentils in water with turmeric and salt for approximately 4 whistles or cook in a vessel for 30 minutes till the ingredients are mixed. Mash this mixture well and keep aside.
2. Wash mince meat and drain out all the water.
3. Heat ghee in a pan, add only the white portion of the chopped spring onions and fry till light golden brown. Add the mince meat, along with ginger and garlic paste and a pinch of turmeric powder and salt to taste.
4. Fry all this together and when the water evaporates and the mince meat is dry, add chopped dill. Then add the chopped green stems of the spring onions and mix into the mince. When the meat begins to stick to the pan, switch off the gas.
5. Take another pan and place on a medium flame. Pour in the cooked rice and dal mixture. Add the meat mixture into this soft mash of rice and dal and mix well.
6. Add the beaten yoghurt into this mince and rice mixture and keep stirring continuously till it begins to boil.
7. Keep cooking till the mince is cooked.
8. Add peppercorns and green chillies and cook on a low flame for 20 minutes.
9. Garnish with fried golden brown onions which have been crushed and sprinkle with mint leaves and serve.

Kofta Salan

Meatball curry

1 kg	Lamb, minced	1 tbsp	Ginger-garlic paste
¼ cup	Yellow split-pea lentil (*channa dal*)	½ tsp	Red chilli (*lal mirch*) powder
½ tsp	Black pepper (*kali mirch*) powder	½ tsp	Turmeric (*haldi*) powder
½ bunch	Fresh coriander	½ tsp	Coriander (*dhania*) powder
14	Green chillies (or as per taste)	½ tsp	Garam masala
3 small	Onions	2 tbsp	Oil
¼	Coconut	1 cup	Yoghurt (*dahi*)
12 to 15	Mint (*pudina*) leaves	1	Lemon, juiced
½ kg	Tomatoes, pureed	Salt to taste	

Method

1. Take mince meat, lentil, black pepper, fresh coriander, 4 green chillies, 1 onion, half of the coconut quantity and grind into a fine paste.

2. Make this paste into small balls, deep fry and keep aside.

3. Separately grind 2 onions, the remaining coconut, 6 green chillies, a few mint leaves, along with some garam masala and keep aside.

4. Grind tomatoes into a paste.

5. Heat the oil in a pan and fry all the groud mixture of Step 3 along with ginger-garlic paste, red chilli powder, turmeric and coriander powder. Then add salt and the tomato puree and simmer.

6. Stir well, then add beaten yoghurt and lime juice.

7. Stir in ½ glass of water and cook for some more time.

8. Lastly, add the fried kebabs and cook for 10 minutes on slow fire.

9. Sprinkle fresh coriander and 4 half-slit green chillies and keep on slow fire for another 5 minutes till the oil rises to the top of the pan and serve.

Sabzi Gosht

Lamb cooked with vegetables

Serves: 8

Ingredients

1 kg	Mutton, pieces	½ tsp	Garam masala
4	Potatoes, cut	2 large	Onions, sliced
½ kg	French beans	2 tsp	Ginger-garlic paste
2	Tomatoes, sliced	½ tsp	Turmeric (*haldi*) powder
2 bundles	Dill (*sui ki bhaji*)	1 tsp	Coriander (*dhania*) powder
2 bundles	Fenugreek (*methi*) leaves	2 tsp	Red chilli (*lal mirch*) powder
½	Coconut, grated	1	Lemon, juiced
¼ bunch	Fresh coriander	Salt to taste	
2 tbsp	Oil		

Method

1. Heat oil in a pan, fry the garam masala and onions together till brown.
2. Add ginger-garlic paste, turmeric, coriander, red chilli powder and mix well.
3. After 5 minutes, when the masala is cooked, add the mutton pieces along with salt to taste. Keep frying for another 10 minutes, till the mutton is well browned.
4. Then add the tomatoes and fry till they are mixed well with rest of the ingredients.
5. Add 1 cup of water and add the potatoes and beans into the pan.
6. Let this simmer for 10 minutes.
7. Stir in the dill and fenugreek.
8. After another 10 minutes or so, when all this comes to a boil, add a little grated coconut and mix well.
9. After 5 minutes, lower the flame, add the coriander and the lemon juice.
10. Leave to cook on slow fire for another 5 minutes. Serve.

Aloo Gosht

Mutton with potatoes

Serves: 6

Ingredients

1 kg	Mutton/ Lamb	2 tsp	Red chilli (*lal mirch*) powder
3 tbsp	Oil		
4 medium	Onions	¼ bunch	Fresh coriander (*dhania pata*) leaves
6	Garlic cloves		
1"	Ginger	6 to 8 half slit	Green chillies
5	Potatoes, half-boiled and cut in half	½ tsp	Garam masala
		Salt to taste	
½ tsp	Turmeric (*haldi*) powder		

Method

1. Grind together the onions, garlic and ginger.

2. Fry this paste in oil till it becomes light brown.

3. Mash two half-boiled potatoes and add to the paste.

4. Now put in the meat with ½ cup of water.

5. Cover the pan and keep on slow flame till all the water dries up. Then increase the flame and fry the meat, adding salt to taste, turmeric and red chilli powder.

6. Next, keep frying till the meat mixture is dry.

7. Then add 2 to 3 glasses of water and keep on a high flame till the meat becomes very tender.

8. Once the meat is cooked, lower the flame and add the remaining half-boiled potatoes.

9. If you require extra gravy then add a little water, but keep the flame low.

10. Add some fresh coriander and half-slit green chillies and cook on slow fire for 5 more minutes.

11. Before serving, sprinkle some garam masala on top.

Cabbage Mutton

Slow-cooked mutton curry with cabbage

Serves: 8-10

1 kg	Mutton
1½kg	Cabbage (*bandh gobhi*)
¼ kg	Onions, roughly chopped
¼ kg	Tomatoes, roughly chopped
¼	Dry coconut, grated
2 tbsp	Oil
2 tsp	Ginger-garlic paste
2 tsp	Red chilli (*lal mirch*) powder
¼ tsp	Turmeric (*haldi*) powder
1 tsp	Coriander (*dhania*) powder
¼ bunch	Fresh coriander (*dhania pata*)
6 to 8 half slit	Green chillies
Salt to taste	

1. Heat oil in a pan and fry the meat with ginger-garlic paste, onions, red chilli powder, turmeric powder, coriander powder and salt to taste. Add a full glass of water when the masala is brown and allow the meat to cook on high flame and cover the pan.

2. When the water dries up, allow the meat to fry for a few minutes in its own steam. Add tomatoes and fry till they are cooked.

3. Add the cabbage to the meat, along with the grated coconut.

4. Lower the flame and cook till the cabbage is done.

5. Sprinkle coriander and green chillies and leave to cook on slow fire for 5 more minutes and serve.

Mutton Dhansak with Brown Rice

Parsi mutton and lentil stew, with brown rice

Ingredients

1 kg	Mutton
3	Onions, finely chopped
2 tbsp	Oil
1 tsp	Cumin (jeera) seeds
1 tsp	Ginger paste
1 tsp	Garlic paste
2	Tomatoes, chopped
100 gm	Pigeon pea lentils (*tuwar dal*)
100 gm	Split red lentils (*masoor dal*)
50 gm	Split yellow dal (*moong dal*)
3 tbsp	Dhansak masala (see below for recipe)
50 gm	Tamarind (*imli*) or juice of 1 lemon
¼ bunch	Fresh coriander (*dhania pata*) leaves
Salt to taste	

Dhansak Masala:

100 gm	Coriander (*dhania*) seeds
50 gm	Fenugreek (*methi dana*) seeds
50 gm	Mustard (*sarson*) seeds
50 gm	Cumin (*jeera*) seeds
50 gm	Bay Leaves (*tej pata*)
100 gm	mixed cardamom (*elaichi*), cloves (*laung*) and cinnamon (*dalchini*)

Preparing Dhansak Masala:

1. Place a frying pan on high flame. When hot, add the coriander seeds, fenugreek, mustard seeds, bay leaves, cardamom, cloves, cinnamon and dry roast till slightly brown. Let it cool.

2. Place all the ingredients in a grinder and make a fine powder mixture. Bottle this in a jar.

3. This is known as Dhansak masala.

4. Heat oil in a large deep pan. Add onions along with cumin and fry till light brown.

5. Then add ginger-garlic paste and 3 tablespoons of the prepared dhanshak masala along with turmeric, chilly powder, tomatoes. Keep frying till the tomatoes are dissolved and blended with the onions.

6. Once done, remove the pan from the heat.

7. In a pressure cooker, add the mutton pieces and 1 litre water along with the three kinds of lentils. Add salt to taste and pressure cook till 2 whistles of the cooker.

8. Pour the mutton and dal mixture from the cooker into the previously prepared masala and mix all of this together.

9. Add some tamarind water or lime juice, coriander leaves and cook on slow fire for 10 to 15 minutes and then serve.

Favourite
Simone Arora, my second daughter
can't get enough of the mutton
dhansak with
brown rice and kebabs.

Parsi-Style Mutton Curry

Mutton and potato curry with Parsi spices

Serves: 8

Ingredients

1 kg	Mutton, cut into pieces	1 tsp	Turmeric (*haldi*) powder
4	Potatoes, cut into quarters	1 tsp	Red chilli (*lal mirch*) powder
1 tsp	Ginger paste	½	Coconut, grated
1½ tsp	Garlic paste	1 cup	Coconut Milk
10	Red Kashmiri chillies (*sabut Kashmiri lal mirch*)	3	Onions, sliced
		10	Curry leaves
2 tsp	Each of cumin (*jeera*) seeds, sesame (*til*) seeds, poppy (*khus khus*) seeds and coriander (*dhania*) seeds	2	Bay leaves
		1	Lemon, juiced
		Salt to taste	
10 cloves	Garlic	4 tbsp	Oil

Method

1. Heat oil in a pan. Fry the mutton pieces until brown with ginger and garlic paste and salt.

2. In a cooker, add the mutton and a little water and cook till tender.

3. Grind Kashmiri chillies, cumin, sesame, poppy, coriander, garlic, turmeric, red chilli powder, and grated coconut. Keep aside.

4. Fry the onion till light brown. Then add the ground masala (step 3) and fry together with salt to taste, curry leaves, and bay leaves.

5. After the masala is well-fried, add the mutton along with its stock. Do not add any plain water. Instead, add the required coconut milk for the gravy and simmer.

6. Boil the potatoes and add to the curry as it simmers (if more gravy is required, add some more coconut milk).

7. Finally, stir in the lemon juice and serve.

Sali Boti

Parsi mutton delicacy served with potato straws

Serves: 8

1 kg	Meat pieces	1 tsp	Chilli (*lal mirch*) powder
2	Potatoes, mashed	½ tsp	Turmeric (*haldi*) powder
2 large	Onions, sliced	½ tsp	Cumin (*jeera*) powder
2	Dried red Kashmiri chillies (*sabut Kashmiri lal mirch*)	1 large	Tomato, finely chopped
		3 tbsp	Vinegar
1 piece	Bay Leaf (*tej pata*)	2 tsp	Sugar
3 to 4	Cloves (*laung*)	½ kg	Potatoes to make straws (*sali*)
1 tsp	Garlic paste		Salt to taste
1 tsp	Ginger paste		Oil for frying
1 tsp	Coriander (*dhania*) powder		

1. Fry onions till light brown. Then add the Kashmiri chillies, bay leaf and cloves.

2. Add the meat pieces along with garlic-ginger paste, coriander and red chilli powder, turmeric and cumin. Fry this and then add finely chopped tomato.

3. After the tomato is mashed in, transfer it to a pressure cooker with a little water.

4. When the meat is cooked, remove and cook on a slow fire.

5. Boil the potatoes set aside to make potato straws, julienne, and deep fry.

6. Now add vinegar, a little sugar to taste and leave on stove till the oil comes on the top. Put in the potato sallies last whilst serving.

Parsi Pepper Mutton Soup

A thin mutton soup made in Parsi-style

Serves: 8

1 kg	Meat	1 large bunch	Coriander (*dhania pata*) leaves
2 medium-size	Onions, chopped		
3	Tomatoes, sliced	¼ bunch	Mint (*pudina*)
2 tbsp	Ginger-garlic paste	7 to 8 half	Green chillies, slit
4 large	Potatoes, cut into quarters	1 tsp	Ground pepper (*kali mirch*)
4 whole	Black Peppercorns (*sabut kali mirch*)	1	Lemon, juiced
		Salt to taste	
1 tsp	Red chilli powder (*lal mirch*)	3-4 tbsp	Oil
½ tsp	Turmeric (*haldi*) powder		

1. Heat oil and fry chopped onions till light brown.

2. Add 1 large cut potato and fry.

3. When potato is well fried, remove from pan and mash it.

4. Put back in pan. Then add ginger-garlic paste and mutton, with salt to taste.

5. Add 2 glasses of water to the meat for a soupy gravy.

6. Leave the meat to simmer till the mutton is half done.

7. Then add 3 cut potatoes, sliced tomatoes, turmeric, freshly ground black pepper and slit green chillies.

8. Simmer till the meat is tender.

9. Lastly, add some mint leaves, fresh coriander, ground pepper along with the juice of lemon and leave this on slow fire for 5 more minutes. Serve.

Aab Gosht

Kashmiri Mutton Curry

Serves: 6-8

Ingredients

1 kg	Mutton, cut into medium pieces	1½ tbsp	Ginger–garlic paste
150 gm	Yellow split pea lentils (*channa dal*)	1 tsp	Turmeric (*haldi*) powder
		1 tsp	Coriander (*dhania*) powder
1 bunch	Spring onions (*harra pyaz*)	2 tsp	Red chilli (*lal mirch*) powder
2 tbsp	Oil	1	Tomato, finely chopped
4	Cloves (*laung*)	1 tsp	Fresh coriander (*dhania pata*),
4	Cardamoms (*elaichi*)		chopped
4"	Cinnamon (*dalchini*)	6	Cherry tomatoes
4	Onions, chopped	Salt to taste	

Method

1. Heat oil in a pan. Add cloves, cardamoms, and cinnamon.
2. Add onions, fry till light brown.
3. Add ginger–garlic paste and meat, fry together for 15 minutes.
4. Add salt to taste, turmeric, coriander powder, red chilli powder. Stir and keep frying.
5. Add chopped tomato. When well stirred, add 2 glasses hot water and cover the pan. Place on medium flame till mutton is half cooked.
6. Add the lentils, chopped green onions and cherry tomatoes and keep cooking till the lentils are cooked through and the mutton is tender.
7. Add fresh coriander and mix.
8. Cover and leave to cook on slow fire till the oil rises to the top.

Dum Ka Kheema

Slow cooked mince meat

Serves: 6-8

Ingredients

1 kg	Mince lamb (*kheema*)
4 tbsp	Oil
4	Cardamoms (*elaichi*), 2" Cinnamon (*dalchini*), 3-4 cloves (*laung*)
5	Onions, chopped
1 tsp	Turmeric (*haldi*) powder
2½ tsp	Red chilli (*lal mirch*) powder
1½ tsp	Coriander (*dhania*) powder
2 tsp	Ginger-garlic paste
½ kg	Tomatoes, chopped
5 to 6	Green chillies, chopped
¼ bunch	Fresh coriander (*dhania pata*) leaves
1	Lemon, juiced
Salt to taste	

Method

1. Wash mince and keep aside.
2. In a pan, heat oil.
3. Add cardamom, cinnamon, cloves, onions and fry till light brown.
4. Add the mince to the pan.
5. Add turmeric, red chilli powder, coriander powder, garlic-ginger paste. Stir well with the mince. Fry till the liquid in the mince evaporates.
6. Add tomatoes and fry on high flame till the tomatoes become mushy.
7. Add half cup of water, cover the pan and simmer on high flame till done.
8. Once done, lower the flame, add green chillies, coriander and lemon juice.
9. Lower the flame and leave to cook on slow fire for 7 to 8 minutes.
10. Serve with paratha.

Peshawari Kheema

A rich spiced dry mincemeat preparation.
The sliced ginger is typical to the frontier style of cooking.

Serves: 8-10

1 kg	Mince mutton (*kheema*)
2 tbsp	Ghee
1 tsp	Garam masala
1" finely cut	Ginger slices
6-8 flakes	Garlic
2 tsp	Red chilli (*lal mirch*) powder
2 big	Tomatoes, sliced
5 to 6	Green chillies, slit
½ bunch	Fresh coriander (*dhania pata*)
Salt to taste	

Method

1. Heat ghee and fry the mince lamb for 6 to 8 minutes.
2. Then add garam masala, finely chopped ginger, sliced garlic along with red chilli powder. Fry together.
3. Then add sliced tomatoes and mix well and cook till the mince is done.
4. Add green chillies and fresh coriander to the meat and leave on slow fire to simmer for 5 to 6 minutes.
5. Then serve.

Mutton Korma

Mutton cooked in a rich yoghurt gravy   *Serves: 6-8*

1 kg	Mutton	½ kg	Yoghurt (*dahi*)
6 medium size	Onions, sliced	4 Large	Potatoes, cut
½ tsp	Garam Masala	¼ cup	Fresh coriander (*dhania pata*), finely chopped
½ tsp	Turmeric (*haldi*) powder		
1 tsp	Coriander (*dhania*) powder	6	Green chillies, slit
1½ tsp	Red chilli powder	3-4 tbsp	Oil
1 tsp	Ginger paste	Salt to taste	
1½ tsp	Garlic paste		

1. Fry onions to darkish brown without burning them.

2. Remove from oil and keep aside.

3. In the same oil, add garam masala, black pepper corns, turmeric, coriander and red chilli powder, ginger-garlic paste, salt to taste.

4. Fry this together till the oil comes on top.

5. Now add the mutton pieces and keep frying till all the liquid from the mutton dries up in the pan.

6. Then add the yoghurt and allow it to saturate and mix well with mutton.

7. Now take the fried onion and crush it to a fine powder (preferably by hand) and place this over the mutton.

8. Fry for 2 to 3 minutes more and then add enough hot water to cook the mutton and to create some gravy for the korma.

9. Bring to a boil and then lower the heat and simmer on slow heat till the meat is well done. (If required, add some cut potatoes into the pan when the meat is half-cooked and let it simmer together).

10. When done, garnish with coriander and a few slit green chillies.

11. Serve with an Indian hard bread like Brun Pav or Kadak Pav.

Meat Khichra

Slow cooked lentil and mutton

Serves: 10-12

¼ kg	Yellow split pea (*channa dal*)	1 tsp	Turmeric (*haldi*) powder
¼ kg	Black gram (*urad dal*)	3 tsp	Red chilli (*lal mirch*) powder
¼ kg	Pink lentils (*masoor dal*)	2 tsp	Dry coriander (*dhania*) powder
¼ kg	Split green gram (*moong dal*)	4 large	Tomatoes
¼ kg	Rice	2 tsp	Ground garam masala
1 kg	Soaked wheat (*gehu*)		Half-slit chillies
2 kg	Meat, cut into pieces with bone	½ bunch	Fresh coriander
4 large	Onions, sliced	¼ bunch	Mint (*pudina*) leaves
1 large stick	Cinnamon (*dalchini*)	2 large	Lemon, juiced
4	Cardamoms (*elaichi*)	3-4 tbsp	Oil
6	Cloves (*laung*)		Salt to taste
2 tbsp	Ginger-garlic paste		

Method

1. Cook all the lentils and rice together in a glass of water with salt to taste.

2. When done, mash this together and keep aside.

3. Take soaked wheat (preferably soaked overnight) and pressure cook it till done, approximately 4 whistles, and then mash in a liquidiser and keep aside.

4. In a pan, fry onions till light brown along with the cinnamon, cardamom and clove.

5. Add the washed meat along with ginger-garlic paste, turmeric, red chilli powder, coriander powder. Fry till the meat is browned.

6. Then add the tomatoes and cook till well-blended with the rest.

7. Add a little water into this to allow the meat to cook and become tender (you can also pressure cook this if necessary).

8. Once the meat is tender, mix the lentils and wheat mixture into it and cook together.

9. Leave it on slow fire to cook for about 5 to 8 minutes. Add some ground garam masala, a few half slit green chillies, cut coriander, mint leaves and lemon juice.

10. When serving, garnish with crisp golden fried onions over the mixture and slices of lemon on the side. Serve with kachumbar salad (see page 185).

Favourite

My grandson Armaan, son of Simone
and Ajay Arora loves Meat Khichra.

Red Masala Chops

Fried mutton chops in a red marinade

Ingredients

1 kg	Mutton chops
2 tsp	Red chilli (*lal mirch*) powder
½ tsp	Turmeric (*haldi*) powder
2 tsp	Ginger-garlic paste
1	Lemon, juiced
Oil for frying	
Salt to taste	

Method

1. Wash the chops and marinate in red chilli powder, turmeric powder, ginger-garlic paste and salt to taste.

2. Marinate for half an hour. Then place the chops and the marinade in a pan, adding just enough water for the chops to become tender while boiling.

3. Once the water has dried up and the mutton is cooked, add oil in the pan to deep fry the chops till it takes on a nice deep red colour and the masala is coating the chops.

4. Pour the lemon juice over the chops and serve.

Potato Chop

Potato croquettes stuffed with mutton

Serves: 8-10

Ingredients

1 kg	Mutton chops, half boiled
1½ kg	Boiled potatoes, peeled
3 tbsp	Oil
1	Egg, beaten
1 cup	Bread crumbs

To be Ground:

1 small bunch	Fresh coriander (*dhania pata*) leaves
½ bunch	Mint (*pudina*) leaves
6	Green chillies
1 tbsp	Black pepper (*kali mirch*) powder
1	Lemon, juiced
Salt to taste	

Method

1. Heat oil in a pan, add the ground mixture into it, then add the chops and 250 ml water.
2. Cook till chops are tender and the water has evaporated.
3. Mash the potatoes. Add salt to taste.
4. Coat the chops with the mashed potatoes.
5. Dip in beaten egg and bread crumbs.
6. Deep fry till golden brown and serve.

Pepper Chops

Mutton chops in a pepper and tomato gravy

Serves: 8-10

Ingredients

1 kg	Mutton chops
20	Peppercorns
6	Green chillies
1 tbsp	Garlic Paste
1	Lemon, juiced
1 tbsp	Oil
2	Tomatoes, sliced
Salt to taste	

Method

1. Take peppercorns, garlic paste, salt to taste and grind all in a blender along with the juice of the lemon.

2. Marinate the chops in this masala for 1 to 2 hours.

3. Heat oil in a pan, add the marinated meat chops and fry for 5 minutes.

4. Then take the sliced tomatoes and spread evenly over the chops.

5. Cover the pot and simmer for about 1 hour till the meat is tender.

6. If there's too much gravy and you want to dry it further, put the flame on high.

7. When done, serve with bread buns or roti/naan.

Tomato Chops

Mutton chops cooked in a tomato gravy

Serves: 8-10

Ingredients

1 kg	Mutton chops
4 tbsp	Oil
6	Onions, cut in round rings
6	Tomatoes, cut in round rings
1½ tsp	Red chilli (*lal mirch*) powder
½ bunch	Coriander (*dhania pata*) leaves
6 to 8	Green chillies, slit
Salt to taste	

Method

1. Heat oil in a pan. Add the chops and cook on a high flame till the chops are half brown and set aside.

2. In a bowl, mix onions, tomatoes and red chilli powder.

3. Heat oil in a pan, and fry this mixture. Add the half browned chops and cook on high flame for 5 minutes.

4. Lower heat, add salt to taste, and simmer for another 30 minutes till the meat cooks in the tomato and onion juices and becomes tender.

5. When the oil rises to the top, add the coriander and the chillies and leave on slow fire for 5 more minutes and serve.

Methi Chops

Lamb chops cooked with fenugreek

Serves: 8-10

Ingredients

1 kg	Mutton chops
400 gm	Yoghurt (*dahi*)
2 large	Onions, sliced
10 cloves	Garlic, chopped
1"	Ginger, finely sliced
1 bunch	Fenugreek (*methi*), finely chopped
2	Tomatoes, finely chopped
½ tsp	Turmeric (*haldi*) powder
1½ tsp	Chilli (*lal mirch*) powder
1 tsp	Coriander (*dhania*) powder
½ tsp	Garam masala
3-4 tbsp	Oil
Salt to taste	

Method

1. Marinate chops in yoghurt for 30 minutes.
2. Fry onions till golden brown along with garlic and thinly-sliced ginger.
3. Add the mutton chops and fenugreek leaves and cook on a high flame till the oil rises to the top of the pan.
4. Add the tomatoes along with turmeric, chilli, coriander powder and salt.
5. Cover the pan and simmer till the chops are tender.
6. Put some water on the lid of the covered pan as well. This is an important step in the preparation of dry dishes.
7. When the meat is ready, add the garam masala.
8. Keep the pan covered and cook on slow fire for 5 minutes and then serve.

Kachhe Kheema ke Kebabs

Mincemeat kebabs

Serves: 4-6

Ingredients

¼ kg	Mince lamb
1	Onion, finely chopped
2	Green chillies
1 tbsp	Coriander (*dhania pata*) leaves, finely chopped
1 tbsp	Mint (*pudina*) leaves, finely chopped
1 tsp	Black pepper (*kali mirch*), ground
½ tsp	Ginger paste
½ tsp	Garlic paste
1	Egg White
2 slice	White Bread
1	Lemon, juiced
4	Slit green chillies

Mint leaves for garnish

Salt to taste

Oil for frying

Method

1. Mix onion, green chillies, coriander leaves, mint leaves, garlic paste, ginger paste, ground black pepper with the mince lamb along with salt to taste.

2. Soak the slice of white bread in a little water, squeeze out all the water from it and mix this into the meat mixture along with an egg white.

3. Form small balls of this mixture.

4. Heat oil in a frying pan and deep fry these meat balls for 10 to 15 minutes on medium fire.

5. Lower the heat and cook till they are brown.

6. Serve with lime juice, 4 sliced green chillies and mint leaves.

Shammi Kebabs

Mincemeat kebabs

Serves: 6-8

Ingredients

½ kg	Mince lamb (*kheema*)	2 each	Cloves (*laung*), Cinnamon (*dalchini*), Cardamom (*elaichi*)
100 gm	Yellow split pea lentils (*channa dal*)		
5	Dried red chillies (*sabut lal mirch*)	2	Tomatoes, chopped
		1 tsp	Turmeric (*haldi*) powder
10 cloves	Garlic	2 chopped	Green chillies
¼ bunch	Coriander (*dhania pata*) leaves	2	Egg whites
		1	Lime
½ bunch	Mint (*pudina*)	Salt to taste	
1	Onion, cut into half	Oil for frying	
1	Potato		

Method

1. In a pan, place mince meat, yellow split pea lentils, red chillies, garlic, coriander, onion, salt, cloves, cinnamon, cardamom, tomatoes, turmeric and green chillies. Add sufficient water and place on a high flame. When the water evaporates completely and the meat and lentil are tender, grind the entire mixture to a sticky consistency. (If possible, use a stone grinder.)

2. Take the egg whites and mix into the meat. Form flat large coin-sized flat cakes (kebabs) and leave aside.

3. Now take a frying pan and pour a very small quantity of oil.

4. When the oil is piping hot, take the kebabs and place gently on the pan.

5. When one side is browned, turn on to the other side and brown gently for a minute or two till done.

6. Before serving, squeeze the lime over the kebabs.

Tinda Mutton

Apple gourd cooked with mutton

Serves: 6-8

Ingredients

1 kg	Mutton pieces
½ kg small	Apple Gourd (*tinda*), whole
5 to 6	Onions, sliced
3	Cloves (*laung*), 3 cardamoms (*elaichi*), 2" Cinnamon (*dalchini*)
3 tsp	Ginger-garlic paste
2 tsp	Chilli (*lal mirch*) powder
1 tbsp	Coriander (*dhania*) powder
½ tsp	Turmeric (*haldi*)
3	Tomatoes, finely chopped
5 to 6	Green chillies, whole
1 cup	Yoghurt (*dahi*)
½ bunch	Fresh coriander (*dhania pata*) leaves
½ tsp	Garam masala
3 tbsp	Oil
Salt to taste	

Method

1. Mix yoghurt and 2 tsp ginger-garlic paste. Marinate the mutton in this mixture for at least 30 minutes.

2. Heat oil in a pan. Add cloves, cardamom, cinnamon. Then add onions.

3. When the onions turn slightly pink, add the remaining garlic-ginger paste, turmeric, coriander powder, red chilli powder and salt. Mix well.

4. Add the marinated mutton and stir fry for 5 minutes. Add chopped tomatoes and cook on high flame till they are well mashed. Add, apple gourd, one glass of water and cook on medium flame.

5. Add green chillies, coriander, garam masala and salt to taste. Cook on low flame for half an hour.

Aloo Kheema Pattice

Potato and mince patty

Makes: 10-12

1 kg	Potatoes, mashed
½ kg	Mince mutton (*kheema*)
3	Onions, chopped
3 tbsp	Oil
3 each	Cloves (*laung*), Cardamom (*elaichi*), Cinnamon (*dalchini*)
1 tbsp	Ginger-garlic paste
1 tsp	Turmeric (*haldi*) powder
1 tbsp	Coriander (*dhania*) powder
1 tbsp	Chilli (*lal mirch*) powder
½ kg	Tomatoes, chopped
½ bunch	Fresh coriander (*dhania pata*) leaves
1 tsp	Garam masala
2	Eggs
Salt to taste	

1. Boil potatoes, remove skin and mash it. Add salt to taste, keep aside.

2. Heat oil in a pan, fry cloves, cinnamon, cardamom, onion and cook till light brown.

3. Add ginger-garlic paste, turmeric powder, coriander powder and red chilli powder.

4. Add mince lamb and mix well.

5. Next add tomatoes and cook till the meat is well cooked.

6. Add fresh coriander and garam masala.

7. Lower the flame and cook till done (no water to be added). Cool this mixture.

8. Take small balls of mashed potato, flatten it on your palm, place a spoon of mince mixture in the middle of the mashed potato and form into a round pattice.

9. Roll the pattice in beaten egg and fry till light brown and serve.

Shikampur Kebab

Stuffed kebabs

Serves: 10-12

Ingredients

1 kg	Mutton, boneless
200 gm	Yellow Split Pea Lentil (*channa dal*)
8	Black Peppercorns (*kali mirch*)
5	Red Kashmir Chillies (*sabut lal mirch*)
1 bunch	Coriander (*dhania pata*) leaves
1	Onion, sliced
2 tbsp	Oil
1 tbsp	Garlic-ginger paste
6	Green chillies
1	Lemon
10 to 15	Mint (*pudina*) leaves
Salt to taste	

Method

1. In a pressure cooker, heat oil. Add mutton pieces, lentils, black peppercorns, Kashmiri chillies, coriander, onion, garlic-ginger paste, salt to taste and 250 ml water and cook for 20 minutes.

2. Then remove all the water from the pan, and grind the meat mixture in a mixer or on a stone grinder.

3. Make shallow cups from the meat mixture and put a stuffing of a kachumber salad (see page 185) of onions, green chillies, lemon, and cover this with another shallow cup made of the meat mixture and form an elongated kebab.

4. Then shallow fry and serve with fresh mint leaves.

Green Masala Mutton

Mutton cooked with a mint-coriander marinade

Serves: 8-10

Ingredients

1 kg	Mutton, cut into approximately 14 pieces
2 large	Onions, sliced
1 tsp	Garlic paste
1 tsp	Ginger paste
2	Lemons, juiced
1 tsp	Garam masala
2	Onions, cut into round slices
3-4 tbsp	Oil
Salt to taste	

For the paste

8	Green chillies
½ bunch	Coriander (*dhania pata*) leaves
10 to 12	Mint (*pudina*) leaves

Method

1. Fry onions till light brown.
2. Add the meat pieces with the garlic-ginger paste and salt. Fry till the masala is cooked.
3. Add the ground paste into the meat.
4. Keep frying till the masala is well-mixed.
5. Then transfer this to a pressure cooker with about ½ cup of water.
6. When mutton is tender, put it back into the pan and let it simmer on a low flame till the oil separates.
7. Add the lime juice, round sliced onions and garam masala. Serve.

Tomato Mirchi Gosht

Mutton cooked with tomatoes and chillies

Serves: 8-10

Ingredients

1 kg	Mutton pieces
2	Onions, chopped
2 to 3	Cardamom (*elaichi*), Cloves (*laung*) and Cinnamon (*dalchini*)
1 tsp	Ginger paste
1 tsp	Garlic paste
2 tsp	Red chilli (*lal mirch*) powder
½ tsp	Turmeric (*haldi*) powder
1 tsp	Coriander (*dhania*) powder
1 tbsp	Coconut powder (optional)
2 kg	Tomatoes, chopped
7 to 8	Green chillies, sliced in half
¼ bunch	Chopped coriander (*dhania pata*) leaves
1	Lemon, juiced
3-4 tbsp	Oil
Salt to taste	

Method

1. Fry onions till golden brown along with cardamom, cloves and cinnamon.

2. Add mutton, ginger-garlic paste, red chillies, turmeric, coriander powder, salt and cook on high flame till all the water from the mutton dries up and the oil is seen on top.

3. At this point add the coconut, if you like.

4. Add the tomatoes to the mutton. Keep on a low flame with the pan covered till the meat becomes tender.

5. Do not add any water.

6. Sprinkle the slit chillies, chopped coriander, lemon juice and leave on slow fire for 5 minutes and then serve.

Paya

Trotters in a lightly spiced gravy

Serves: 15-20

Ingredients

3 dozen	Trotters (*payas*)	3 tsp	Red chilli (*lal mirch*) powder
7 large	Onions, finely chopped	3 tsp	Coriander (*dhania powder*)
4 to 5 tbsp	Oil	2 kg	Tomatoes, pureed
6 to 8	Cardamoms (*elaichi*)	1 bunch	Fresh coriander (*dhania pata*), finely chopped
6	Cloves (*laung*)		
6 pieces	Cinnamon (*dalchini*)	½ bundle	Mint (*pudina*) leaves
3 tbsp	Ginger-garlic paste	Salt to taste	
1 tsp	Turmeric (*haldi*) powder		

Method

1. Place the trotters in a pressure cooker with enough water and cook for 10 whistles (approximately 20 minutes).

2. Next, turn off the flame and let the cooker cool for 30 minutes (don't open the lid of the cooker before that) so that the soup in the cooker thickens.

3. In a large pan, heat oil, and fry cardamom, clove and cinnamon. After a minute or two add the onions and fry till light brown.

4. Then add ginger-garlic paste, turmeric, red chilli powder, coriander, salt and fry all this together with the onions for about 10 more minutes.

5. Open the cooker and remove the trotters. Mix this into the onion masala and fry for 15 minutes.

6. Pour the tomato puree into the pan, stir well and keep frying till the oil comes on top.

7. Pour the thickened gravy from the cooker into the trotters and mix well.

8. Add fresh coriander, mint leaves and stir.

9. Cover the pan and leave to cook on slow fire

10. Keep stirring occasionally so the mixture does not burn.

11. If you need extra gravy, add a little warm water.

12. Once the trotters have softened they are ready to serve.

Hyderabadi Dalcha

Mutton slow-cooked with lentils

Serves: 8

Ingredients

1 kg	Mutton pieces
250 gms	Split red lentil (*masoor* dal)
250 gms	Yellow split pea (*channa* dal)
1 tsp	Tamarind (*imli* – whole)
4 tbsp	Oil
2	Onions
1 tbsp	Ginger-garlic paste
½ tsp	Turmeric powder (*haldi* powder)
2 tbsp	Red chilli powder (*lal mirch* powder)
4	Green chillies
½ bunch	Fresh coriander (*dhania pata*)
2 tbsp	Ghee
4 whole	Dried red chillies (*sabut lal mirch*)
15	Curry leaves
4 peeled	Garlic cloves
½ tsp	Cumin seeds (*jeera* seeds)
½ tsp	Mustard seeds (*sarson* seeds)
Salt to taste	

Method

1. Pressure-cook *masoor* dal and *channa* dal with 4 glasses of water for 3 whistles.

2. Soak tamarind in a cup of water for 15 minutes, deseed, strain the water and keep aside.

3. Simultaneously, heat oil in a heavy base pan, add some *garam masala*, after 2 minutes add the onions and fry till light brown.

4. Add ginger-garlic paste, salt, turmeric, red chilli powder and fry together.

5. Sprinkle a little water if needed to bring out the flavour of the spices. Mix well.

6. Now add the washed mutton and fry till all the water dries up.

7. Pressure cook mutton with just enough water to make it tender.

8. When the meat is ready, add the tenderised dal and the tamarind water, some green chillis, cut fresh coriander and simmer on slow fire for 10 minutes.

9. In a separate frying pan, heat ghee. Add dried red chillies, curry leaves, garlic cloves, cumin, and mustard seeds. After the mixture starts spluttering, and the chillies darken, add this *baghar* into the dal and meat pan and quickly cover the pan with a lid.

10. Serve with white rice and tamarind chutney.

Gurda Fry or Kaleji Fry

Kidney or Liver fry

Ingredients

1 dozen	Kidneys or livers (*gurdas* or *kaleji*), cut into half
4	Tomatoes, finely chopped
4 tbsp	Oil
2	Onions, chopped
5	Green chillies, chopped
¼ bunch	Coriander (*dhania pata*) leaves
½ tsp	Turmeric (*haldi*) powder
2 tsp	Red chilli powder
1½ tsp	Garam masala
1	Lemon, juiced
Salt to taste	

Method

1. Heat oil in a pan. Add the kidneys and salt to taste and fry till all the liquid from the kidneys evaporates.

2. Add turmeric, red chilli powder, onions, green chillies, coriander and fry well.

3. Add some garam masala into this while frying.

4. When the oil comes to the top and the kidneys are cooked, squeeze lemon over it and serve.

If using Liver (kaleji) fry all the ingredients and lastly fry the liver in this masala for not more than 10 minutes or else the liver will harden.

Irish Stew – Chicken/Mutton

One-pot stew with vegetables and chicken/ mutton

Serves: 6-8

Ingredients

1	Chicken, cut into 8 pieces
200 gm	Green beans
2	Carrots
2	Potatoes, cut into quarter pieces
1	Onion, sliced
8 cmall	Baby onions
250 gms	Cauliflower florets
1 tbsp	Butter
3	Cloves (*laung*)
3	Cardamoms (*elaichi*)
3"	Cinnamon (*dalchini*)
1 tbsp	Flour (*maida*)
1 tsp	Ground Black Pepper (*kali mirch*)
¼ cup	Milk
Salt to taste	

Method

1. Cut the green beans and carrots length-wise. Cut potatoes into 4 pieces.

2. Take a pan and place it on a high flame. Add butter. As it melts, add cloves, cardamoms, cinnamon and then the chicken, green beans and carrots. Cook on slow flame for 10 minutes. Add the sliced onions now.

3. After 10 minutes of frying, mix the flour in 1½ glass of water and pour into the chicken.

4. Add ground black pepper and keep stirring till it boils.

5. Add the baby onions and cauliflower.

6. Then add milk, stir, cover with a lid and leave on slow fire for 20 minutes. Check for seasoning and serve.

Bhuna Gosht

Slow cooked spiced mutton

Serves: 6-8

1 kg	Mutton	50 gm	Yoghurt (*dahi*)
2 large	Onions chopped	½ tsp	Garam masala
1 tsp	Garlic paste	A pinch	Mace (*jawitri*)
1 tsp	Ginger paste	¼ bunch	Fresh coriander
¼ tsp	Turmeric (*haldi*) powder	4 tbsp	Oil
2 tsp	Chilli powder	Salt to taste	
2 medium	Tomatoes		

1. Grind onions into a paste.
2. Put oil in pan, add the onion paste and fry till light brown.
3. Then add the washed meat pieces with salt to taste, turmeric, red chilli powder and ginger-garlic paste.
4. Keep frying the mutton pieces till all the masala is well blended.
5. Then add 1 cup water and mix with the mutton.
6. Put the lid on and simmer for 10 minutes on slow fire.
7. Be sure to check that meat does not burn and let this process go on till meat becomes tender.
8. Add tomatoes and yoghurt. Mix this well and put the lid on the pan and leave on slow fire till the meat is very tender and all the liquid evaporates and the oil separates.
9. Before serving sprinkle garam masala.
10. Add some fresh coriander on top and serve with parathas.

Dal Gosht

Lamb cooked with lentils

Ingredients

1 kg	Mutton		½ kg	Tomatoes, finely cut
300 gm	Split red lentils (*masoor dal*)		¼	Coconut, well ground
2 tsp	Ginger-garlic paste		200 ml	Tamarind (*imli*) water
2 tsp	Red chilli (*lal mirch*) powder		2	Lemons, juiced
¼ tsp	Turmeric (*haldi*) powder		1 bunch	Coriander, fresh
1 tsp	Coriander (*dhania*) powder		6	Green chillies, slit
2	Onions, chopped		Salt to taste	
5 tbsp	Oil			

Method

1. Heat oil in a pan. Add mutton, ginger-garlic paste, red chilli powder, turmeric powder, coriander powder, onions, salt and sauté for 10 minutes. Then add ½ glass of water and leave to cook till the water dries up completely.

2. Fry the mutton in the same pan for 5 minutes and add the lentils and keep frying for another 3 to 5 minutes.

3. Now add the tomatoes along with the coconut.

4. Fry for another 5 minutes and then add 2 glasses of water. Leave to cook on a high flame till the lentils and mutton becomes tender. (You could also use a pressure cooker in which case you would have to cook it for 20 minutes). Add the tamarind water or lemon juice, coriander and slit green chillies. Cook on slow fire for 5 more minutes and serve.

Accompaniments & Suggested Menus

Tomato Chutney

Tomato relish

½ kg Tomatoes, mashed, ¼ tsp Turmeric (*haldi*) and 1 tsp Chilli (*lal mirch*) powder, 1 tsp Fenugreek (*methi*), 1 tsp Cumin (*jeera*) and 1 tsp Mustard (*sarson*) seeds, 3 tbsp Oil, 10 Curry leaves, 1 tsp Crushed peppercorns (*kali mirch*), 1 tsp Rock salt, 10 Coarsely ground garlic, 7 Green chillies, Salt to taste

Method

1. Put the mashed tomatoes in a pan on high flame along with turmeric, chilli powder and salt. Do not add any water.
2. On a girdle, roast fenugreek, cumin, mustard seeds. Grind this mixture finely.
3. In another pan, heat oil and fry curry leaves and crushed pepper. When slightly brown, strain the oil and keep aside.
4. Grind rock salt and roast on a girdle.
5. Fry the fenugreek, cumin, mustard seed mixture along with the roasted rock salt, curry leaves and peppercorns. Add the boiled tomatoes into this mixture and keep frying.
6. Add more chilli, turmeric powder or salt according to your taste.
7. Then add a few pieces of coarsely ground garlic to the tomato mixture and half-slit green chillies and place on slow fire till the oil surfaces on top.

Green Chutney

Coriander relish

Ingredients

½ bunch Fresh coriander (*dhania pata*), ¼ bunch Mint (*pudina*) leaves, 4 Green chillies, 1 tbsp Coconut powder, 2 Lemons, juiced, Salt to taste

Method

1. Grind the above ingredients together.

Mint Chutney

Mint relish

Ingredients

1 Raw mango (*kacchi kairi*), ½ bunch Mint (*pudina*) leaves, 3 or 4 Green chillies, 2 or 3 Walnuts, Salt to taste

Method

1. Peel raw mango and grind it with mint leaves, green chillies, salt and walnuts (if raw mango is not available use tamarind water or vinegar).

Onion Kachumbar
Onion salad

Ingredients

2 Onions, finely cut into rounds and separate, 15 Mint (*pudina*) leaves, 2 Green chillies, ½ tsp Red chilli (*lal mirch powder*), 1 tbsp Vinegar or Lemon, Salt to taste

Method

1. Cut the onions, add salt to taste and leave for ½ hour.
2. Then wash the onions to remove all the salt. Drain the water and keep aside.
3. Cut mint leaves and green chillies and mix with the onions.
4. Add red chilli powder, a pinch of salt and vinegar or the juice of 1 large lemon and serve.

*Add finley chopped tomatoes if desired.

Raita
Whipped spiced yoghurt

Ingredients

1 small Onion, chopped, 1 small Tomato, chopped, 1 small Cucumber, chopped, 1 Green chilli, chopped, ½ kg Yoghurt (*dahi*), Salt to taste

For garnish: 1 tsp Cumin (*jeera*) powder, ½ tsp Red chilli (*lal mirch*) powder, 1 tbsp Coriander (*dhania pata*), chopped

Method

1. Beat the yoghurt and add all the ingredients and salt to taste and mix well. Sprinkle cumin powder, red chilli powder and fresh coriander on top.

Full Mirchi Fry
Fried whole green chillies

Ingredients

250 gm Green chillies, 1 tsp Dry coriander powder, Salt to taste, Oil for frying

Method

1. Slit the green chillies halfway, and fill each with salt and dry coriander powder and leave for 15 minutes to marinate.
2. Fry just before serving.

SUGGESTED MENUS

Mummy's Style Fish Curry Pg 89, Aloo Chakna Pg 35, and White Rice.

Tomato Mirchi Gosht Pg 171, Khichri Pg 68, Chawlai Bhaji Pg 42, and Shammi Kebabs Pg 163.

Sabzi Gosht Pg 131, Dahi Ki Curry Pg 48, Channe Ki Dal Ke Barreh Pg 37, and White Rice.

Mutton Dhansak Pg 137, Brown Rice for Dhansak Pg 69, Kachhe Kheema ke Kebabs Pg 162, and Zulekha Baingan Pg 41.

Kofta Salan Pg 130, Bangalori Dal Pg 47, Stuffed Karelas Pg 33, and White Rice.

Palak Chicken Pg 117, Red Masala Chops Pg 155, and White Rice.

Kalmiri ka Char Pg 31, Red Masala Chops Pg 155, Aloo Mattar Pg 45, and White Rice.

Parsi-Style Mutton Curry Pg 141, Fish Fry in Green Masala Pg 75, and White Rice.

Fish/Prawn Patia Pg 77, Dal Pareen Pg 36, Fish Fry in Green Masala Pg 75, Onion Kachumbar Pg 185, and White Rice.

Red Masala Prawns/Fried Pomfret Pg 81, Bangalori Dal Pg 47, Kalmiri ka Char Pg 31, Onion Kachumbar Pg 185, and White Rice.

Challau Rice Pg 71, Chicken Korma Pg 103, Dahiwala Baingan Pg 29 and Dal Pareen Pg 36.

Crab Curry Pg 94, Aloo Mattar Pg 45, Mint Chutney Pg 184, and White Rice.

Khichri Pg 68, Parsi Fish/Prawn Sauce Pg 87, Aloo Tikki Pg 43, and Chicken Hasina in black pepper Pg 101.

Mutton Biryani Pg 65 or Chicken Biryani Lazeez with Potato Pg 62, Dalcha with Dudhi Pg 49, and Shikampur Kebab Pg 167.

Bhindi Gosht Pg 125, Bangalori Dal Pg 47, and Chicken Liver Pg 112, and White Rice.

White Fish Curry Pg 79, Aloo Mattar Pg 45, Tomato Chops Pg 159, and White Rice.

Kheema Pulau Pg 55, Bagara Baingan Pg 39, Hyderabadi Dalcha Pg 174, and Raita Pg 185.

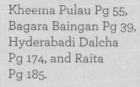

Chicken Green Masala Pg 109, Stuffed Karelas Pg 33, Kalmiri ka Char Pg 31, Bangalori Dal Pg 47, and White Rice.

Chop Pulau Pg 56, Dalcha with Dudhi Pg 49, Onion Kachumbar Pg 185, and Shammi Kebabs Pg 163.

Egg Curry Pg 119, Shammi Kebabs Pg 163, Karai Chicken Pg 111, and White Rice.

SUGGESTED MENUS

Aab Gosht Pg 145 with Kadak Pav, Aloo Tikki Pg 43, and Green Chutney Pg 184.

Sali Chicken Pg 115, Pepper Chops Pg 157, and White Rice.

Sabzi Gosht Pg 131, Dahi ki Curry Pg 48, Channe ki Dal ke Barreh Pg 37, and White Rice.

Prawn Pulau Pg 53, Fish in Green Masala Pg 75, Zulekha Baingan Pg 41, and Raita Pg 185.

Fish Pulau Pg 57, Red Masala Prawns Pg 81, Full Mirchi Fry Pg 185, Bangalori Dal Pg 47 and White Rice.

Dahi Chicken Barbecue Pg 106, Hyderabadi Dalcha Pg 174, Onion Kachumbar Pg 185 Aloo Mattar Pg 45 and White Rice.

Sabzi Gosht Pulau Pg 59, Raita Pg 185, and Red Kachumber Pg 185.

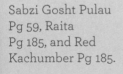

Biryani Masala Rice Pg 61, Chicken Korma Pg 103, Dahiwala Baingan Pg 29, and Methi Chops Pg 161.

Dahi Murg Pg 104, Bhuna Gosht Pg 180, and White Rice.

Prawn Kebabs Pg 83, Tinda Mutton Pg 165, Bagara Baingan Pg 39, and White Rice.

Hyderabadi Prawn Curry Pg 82, Chawlai Bhaji Pg 42, Aloo Tikki Pg 43, and White Rice.

Irish Stew - Chicken/Mutton Pg 179 and Bread Rolls.

Patra Ni Macchi Pg 85, White Fish Curry Pg 79, Green Chutney Pg 184, and White Rice.

Surmai Fry Pg 93, Bangalori Dal Pg 47, Aloo Chakna Pg 35, and Kalmiri ka Char Pg 31.

Chicken Masala Kashmiri Pg 120, Peshawari Kheema Pg 148, Aloo Tikki Pg 43, and White Rice.

Persian Aash Maash Pg 129, Zulekha Baingan Pg 41, and Raita Pg 185.

Aloo Gosht Pg 133, Stuffed Karelas Pg 33, Tomato Chutney Pg 184, Bangalori Dal Pg 47, and White Rice.

Cabbage Mutton Pg 135, Dum ka Kheema Pg 147, Dal Pareen Pg 36, and Aloo Tikki Pg 43.

Green Masala Mutton Pg 169, Bangalori Dal Pg 47, Aloo Chakna Pg 35, and White Rice.

Murg Malai Korma Pg 105, Gurda Fry Pg 177, Bangalori Dal Pg 47, and White Rice.

Index

The Author and Publisher would like to thank GOODEARTH
for all tableware and dining accessories used in the book.

www.goodearth.in

Second impression, 2016

First published by Roli Books in 2015
M-75, Greater Kailash II Market
New Delhi-110 048, India
Phone: ++91-11-4068 2000
Fax: ++91-11-29217185
E-mail: info@rolibooks.com
Website: www.rolibooks.com

ISBN: 978-93-5194-108-8

Editors: Rayman Gill Rai, Priya Kapoor
Photo Editor: Saloni Vaid
Design: Sneha Pamneja
Pre-press: Jyoti Dey
Production: Yuvraj Singh

Printed and bound at Rave India, New Delhi